The Most Frequently Used Lakota Adjectives: Save Time by Learning the Most Frequently Used Words First

John White Eagle

Contents

The Most Frequently Used Lakota Adjectives: Save Time by Learning the Most Frequently Used Words First

John White Eagle

About the Author

John White Eagle is a distinguished American linguist with a profound expertise in the Lakota language. Born and raised in South Dakota, John has dedicated his career to the study and preservation of this Native American language. His language-learning books are celebrated for their comprehensive approach and cultural depth, providing learners with a rich understanding of Lakota grammar, vocabulary, and traditions.

John's work extends beyond authorship; he is actively involved in community initiatives aimed at revitalizing the Lakota language. His contributions have not only educated numerous individuals but also strengthened the cultural heritage of the Lakota-speaking community.

Other Works by This Author

Series: Most Frequently Used Words

Introducing a unique Lakota language book series, prioritizing the most frequently used words. Covering nouns, verbs and adjectives, it's perfect for enhancing spoken and written skills. Words are sorted by frequency, each with English translations and example sentences for comprehensive learning. Ideal for all levels, it's a great tool to master Lakota vocabulary effectively.

1. The Most Frequently Used Lakota Nouns: Save Time by Learning the Most Frequently Used Words First
2. The Most Frequently Used Lakota Adjectives: Save Time by Learning the Most Frequently Used Words First
3. The Most Frequently Used Lakota Verbs: Save Time by Learning the Most Frequently Used Words First

Introduction

Welcome to the enchanting world of Lakota adjectives, the colorful words that paint our conversations and writings with vivid detail and emotion. This book is your comprehensive guide to mastering the most frequently used Lakota adjectives, an essential toolkit for anyone eager to deepen their understanding and use of the language. Adjectives play a crucial role in language, allowing us to describe nouns, giving life to our descriptions, and making our communications more precise and interesting. Whether you're starting your journey into Lakota or looking to enrich your existing skills, this collection of adjectives will expand your ability to express yourself with greater clarity and richness.

Adjectives are the words we use to modify or describe nouns and pronouns, offering additional information about an object's size, shape, age, color, origin, or material, among other qualities. They help us create a vivid picture in the listener's or reader's mind, enhancing our expressions and communications. For example, words like "beautiful," "large," "ancient," and "silky" transform simple sentences into more detailed and engaging narratives. "A beautiful garden," "a large room," "an ancient city," and "silky hair" not only tell us more about the nouns they describe but also evoke feelings and images, making the language more impactful and memorable.

In addition to the rich array of adjectives, this book also introduces you to the most frequently used adverbs, further enriching your vocabulary and expressive capabilities. Adverbs modify verbs, adjectives, or other adverbs, providing additional information about how, when, where, and to what extent an action is performed. For example, "quickly," "very," "yesterday," and "extremely" are adverbs that can describe how fast someone runs, the intensity of a feeling, the timing of an action, and the degree of a quality. By mastering the use of adverbs, you'll be able to convey your thoughts and actions with greater precision and nuance, making your Lakota even more dynamic and expressive.

This book is designed not only to enhance your vocabulary but also to provide you with the tools to use adjectives and adverbs effectively in real-life contexts. Through practical examples and and comprehensive explanations, you'll learn how to select the perfect words to convey your thoughts and emotions accurately. As you progress through the chapters, you'll discover new ways to describe the world around you, enriching your conversations, writings, and understanding of the Lakota language. Let's embark on this colorful journey together, unlocking the power of adjectives and adverbs to make your Lakota more vivid and expressive than ever before.

— John White Eagle

Contents at a Glance

1. Full List

Initially, the words will be presented according to their *frequency of use*: starting with the most frequently used words, then slowly going to the least frequently used words. After this, the words will be organized alphabetically.

In the sections containing example sentences, English translations are provided separately, allowing you to concentrate on deciphering the meaning in English before consulting the provided translations for verification.

---

1. hiyá — *no* — The term 'hiyá' is used to express negation or refusal in Lakota. It can be used in response to questions or statements to indicate disagreement or denial. It is often placed at the beginning of a sentence for emphasis. The context in which it is used can vary, but its primary function remains to convey a negative response.
• Hiyá, waŋbláke šni.
- *No, I didn't see it.*

---

2. šni — *not* — The term 'šni' is used to negate verbs or adjectives in Lakota. It typically follows the word it negates, functioning similarly to 'not' in English. This negation can apply to actions, states, or qualities, providing a straightforward way to express the absence or opposite of something.
• Waŋbláke šni.
- *I do not see it.*

---

3. ičíč'iyapi — *all* — The term 'ičíč'iyapi' is used to denote the concept of 'all' or 'every' in the Lakota language. It is typically placed before the noun it modifies to indicate totality or completeness. This term can be used in various contexts to emphasize that something applies to every member of a group or every part of a whole.
• Ičíč'iyapi wíčhóiye kiŋ héčha.
- *All the words are like that.*

4. heči — *so* — The word 'heči' is used to express a degree or extent, similar to the English word 'so'. It is often used to emphasize the intensity or quality of an adjective or situation. It can be placed before an adjective or adverb to amplify its meaning, providing a stronger emotional or descriptive context.
• Wíyukčaŋ heči waŋží waŋbláke.
- *I saw such a beautiful flower.*

5. iyás'a — *just* — The term 'iyás'a' is used to convey the sense of fairness, exactness, or appropriateness in a situation. It can be applied to describe actions, decisions, or conditions that are deemed to be just or fair. This term helps to emphasize the correctness or suitability of something within a given context.
• Wíyukčaŋ iyás'a kiŋháŋ, wówaši kiŋ wówašte.
- *When the judgment is just, the work is good.*

6. lé — *here* — The term 'lé' is used to indicate the presence or location of something in close proximity to the speaker. It emphasizes that the subject is 'here' or 'in this place.' It can be used in various contexts to point out objects, people, or places that are near the speaker.
• Lé wíyukse kiŋ.
- *Here is the knife.*

7. hé — *there* — The word 'hé' is used to indicate the presence or location of something at a distance from both the speaker and the listener. It functions similarly to the English word 'there' and is often used to point out or draw attention to something that is not immediately close. It helps in providing spatial context within a conversation.
• Hé wíyukse kiŋ.
- *There is the knife.*

8. wóuŋspe — *right* — The term 'wóuŋspe' is used to describe something that is correct or proper. It can be applied in various contexts to indicate correctness, accuracy, or appropriateness-. This term is often used in educational or instructional settings to affirm that something is done correctly or to guide someone towards the correct action or answer.

● Hoksíla kiŋ wóuŋspe táku he?
- *Is the boy right about that?*

---

9. ičámna — *out* — The word 'ičámna' is used to describe something that is outside or not inside a particular space. It can be used to indicate the physical location of an object or person. It is often used in contexts where the position relative to an enclosed space is important.

● Wíyukčaŋ waŋ íčámna hwo?
- *Is the tree outside?*

---

10. iyéna — *up* — The term 'iyéna' is used to describe a direction or position that is elevated or higher in relation to something else. It can be used in various contexts to indicate upward movement or a higher location. It is often paired with verbs or nouns to provide a clearer picture of the spatial relationship being described.

● Wíyukčaŋ iyéna hiyú.
- *The bird flew up.*

---

11. leháŋ — *now* — The term 'leháŋ' is used to indicate the present moment or the current time. It emphasizes immediacy or the current state of affairs. It can be used in various contexts to highlight that something is happening right now or has just occurred.

● Leháŋ wíyukčaŋ waŋží yuhá.
- *Now, I have a question.*

---

12. toháŋ — *how* — The term 'toháŋ' is used to inquire about the manner or condition of something. It seeks to understand the way in which an action is performed or the state of a situation. It is often placed at the beginning of a question to ask

'how' something is done or 'how' something is. This term helps in gathering detailed information about the process or state being questioned.
- Toháŋ hečhíŋ kiŋ hé?
- *How is the weather?*

---

13. t'e — *well* — In Lakota, 't'e' is used to describe a state of being well or in good health. It can be applied to people, animals, or even situations to indicate that everything is in a good condition. The word is versatile and can be used in various contexts to convey wellness or satisfactory status.
- Wičháša t'e.
- *The man is well.*

---

14. kiŋháŋ — *as* — The term 'kiŋháŋ' is used to draw comparisons or to indicate similarity between two entities or actions. It functions similarly to the English word 'as' in comparative contexts. It helps to establish a relationship where one thing is likened to another, emphasizing their similarity or equivalence.
- Wí kiŋháŋ škáŋ šni héčha.
- *The sun is not moving as it should.*

---

15. wašté — *good* — The term 'wašté' is used to describe something positive or of high quality. It can be applied to people, objects, or situations to convey goodness or excellence. It is versatile and can be used in various contexts to express approval or satisfaction.
- Lé wíčazo wašté héčha.
- *This is a good pencil.*

---

16. toké — *why* — The term 'toké' is used to inquire about the reason or purpose behind an action or situation. It seeks to understand the cause or motivation. It is typically placed at the beginning of a question to ask 'why' something is happening or has happened.
- Toké he? Iyéčhiŋkiŋyaŋke kiŋ he?

- Why? Is it the car?

17. tokéya — *when* — The word 'tokéya' is used to inquire about the time or occasion something happens. It functions similarly to the English word 'when'. It can be used in various contexts to ask about past, present, or future events. The placement of 'tokéya' in a sentence typically follows the subject and precedes the verb, maintaining the structure of the Lakota language.
• Niyáŋke tokéya he?
- When did you see it?

18. toká — *where* — The word 'toká' is used to inquire about the location or place of something or someone. It functions similarly to the English word 'where'. It is often placed at the beginning of a sentence to form a question. The context of the sentence will determine the specific nature of the inquiry, whether it is about a person, object, or event.
• Toká he?
- Where is it?

19. heháŋ — *then* — The word 'heháŋ' is used to indicate a sequence of events, similar to 'then' in English. It helps to connect actions or states in a narrative, showing what happens next. It is often placed at the beginning or within a sentence to maintain the flow of events.
• Wíyukčaŋ kiŋ úŋpi kte ló, heháŋ wíčhokaŋ kiŋ yápi kte ló.
- They will eat the food, then they will go to the meeting.

20. k'iŋ — *some* — The term 'k'iŋ' is used to indicate an unspecified quantity or number of something. It can be used to refer to a part of a whole or to some members of a group without specifying which ones. It helps in making general statements or when the exact details are unknown or irrelevant.
• Wíyukse k'iŋ waŋží waŋbláke.
- I see some birds.

21. waníyaŋ — *really* — The term 'waníyaŋ' is used to emphasize the degree or intensity of an action or quality, similar to the English word 'really'. It can be placed before verbs or adjectives to strengthen the statement. It adds emphasis and can convey sincerity or intensity in the speaker's message.

• Waníyaŋ waŋbláke kiŋháŋ, táku waŋží waŋyáŋkapi kte ló.

- *When I really look, I will see something.*

---

22. iyéčhetu — *too* — The word 'iyéčhetu' is used to indicate that something is excessive or more than necessary, similar to the English word 'too'. It can be used to describe various situations where an excess is noted, such as too much of an action, quality, or quantity. It is typically placed before the verb or adjective it modifies to convey the sense of excess.

• Wíyukčaŋ iyéčhetu waŋží waŋbláke.

- *I see one too many stars.*

---

23. tkíŋ — *more* — The term 'tkíŋ' is used to indicate an increase or greater degree of a quality or quantity. It functions similarly to the English word 'more' and is often used in comparative contexts to show that one thing has a greater amount or degree of a particular attribute than another.

• Wíyukčaŋ tkíŋ wóuŋspe ló.

- *She knows more about plants.*

---

24. ištáŋ — *down* — The word 'ištáŋ' is used to describe a direction or position that is lower or beneath something else. It can be used in various contexts to indicate a downward movement or location. It is often paired with verbs or nouns to provide a clearer picture of the spatial relationship.

• Wíyukčaŋ ištáŋ hiyú.

- *The bird flew down.*

---

25. tókšiŋ — *never* — The term 'tókšiŋ' is used to express the concept of 'never' in Lakota. It is typically placed before the verb to indicate that an action has not occurred and will not occur at

any time. This word is useful for emphasizing the impossibility or absolute negation of an event or action.
● Tókšiŋ waŋyáŋkȟe šni.
- *I will never see it.*

---

26. waštéwalake — *very* — The term 'waštéwalake' is used to intensify the meaning of the word it modifies, similar to 'very' in English. It emphasizes the degree or extent of an adjective or adverb, making the description more forceful. It is typically placed before the word it modifies to convey a stronger sentiment or quality.
● Héčha waštéwalake.
- *It is very good.*

---

27. iyápi — *only* — The term 'iyápi' is used to emphasize exclusivity or singularity in a statement. It can be placed before or after the noun or verb it modifies, depending on the desired emphasis. It helps to clarify that the subject or action is the sole focus, excluding others.
● Wíyukčaŋ iyápi wíčhóiye kiŋ.
- *The word is only a flower.*

---

28. kipáhda — *over* — The term 'kipáhda' is used to describe something that is positioned above or over another object or area. It can be used in various contexts to indicate physical placement or metaphorical superiority. It is often placed after the noun it describes to convey the spatial relationship.
● Wíyukse kipáhda táku waŋ bluhá.
- *I have something over the table.*

---

29. číkiya — *little* — The term 'číkiya' is used to describe something that is small in size or quantity. It can be applied to various nouns to convey the idea of 'little' or 'small'. This term is versatile and can be used in different contexts, whether referring to objects, animals, or even abstract concepts. It helps to provide a clearer picture of the subject being discussed by emphasizing

its diminutive nature.
- Wíyaka číkiya waŋbláke.
- *I see a little feather.*

---

30. tokéšiceye — *sorry* — The word 'tokéšiceye' is used to express feelings of regret or sorrow. It can be used in various contexts where one wants to convey an apology or express sympathy. This term is often employed in personal interactions to acknowledge a mistake or to show empathy towards someone's unfortunate situation.
- Tokéšiceye, čhaŋtémawašte šni.
- *I'm sorry, I am not happy.*

---

31. tkáyahaŋ — *off* — The term 'tkáyahaŋ' is used to describe something that is no longer functioning or is in a state of disuse. It can be applied to various contexts, such as machinery, electronics, or even situations where something has ceased to be active or operational.
- Wíyutȟapi kiŋ tkáyahaŋ he?
- *Is the light off?*

---

32. hékta — *even* — The term 'hékta' is used to indicate equality or uniformity in a comparison. It can be applied to describe situations where two or more elements are being compared and found to be the same in some respect. This term helps to emphasize that the elements being compared do not differ in the specified aspect.
- Wíyukčaŋ hékta kiŋháŋ, wíčazo hékta kiŋháŋ.
- *The flowers are even, the pencils are even.*

---

33. híŋhaŋna — *sure* — The word 'híŋhaŋna' is used to express certainty or assurance about a statement or situation. It can be placed before or after the noun it modifies, depending on the emphasis and structure of the sentence. This word helps to convey confidence in the information being shared.
- Híŋhaŋna wíyukčaŋ kiŋ waŋčhíŋyaŋke.

- I am sure that I saw the star.

34. waníyetu — *first* — The word 'waníyetu' is used to denote the concept of 'first' in terms of order or sequence. It can be applied in various contexts, such as describing the first item in a series, the first occurrence of an event, or the first person to do something. It is important to place 'waníyetu' appropriately in the sentence to convey the intended meaning clearly.
• Waníyetu wíčhóiye kiŋ lé héčha.
- This is the first word.

35. heya — *still* — The term 'heya' is used to indicate that something is continuing or remains unchanged over time. It conveys the sense of persistence or continuity. It can be used in various contexts to describe actions, states, or conditions that are ongoing.
• Wíyukčaŋ heya wówaši kiŋ.
- The work is still difficult.

36. owátanna — *again* — The term 'owátanna' is used to indicate the repetition of an action or event. It is typically placed before the verb it modifies to convey the sense of 'again' or 'once more'. This term helps to emphasize that something is happening for a second time or repeatedly.
• Owátanna wíyukčaŋ kiŋhán.
- He/She/They will sing again.

37. héčhetu — *maybe* — The term 'héčhetu' is used to express uncertainty or possibility, similar to the English word 'maybe'. It can be placed at the beginning or end of a sentence to indicate that something is not definite. This word helps convey a sense of doubt or speculation about an event or situation.
• Héčhetu, wičháša kiŋ hí kta hé.
- Maybe, the man will come.

38. mahé — *before* — The word 'mahé' is used to indicate something that occurs earlier in time relative to another event or point in time. It is typically placed before the noun or verb it modifies to convey the sense of precedence. This word helps to establish a temporal relationship between events, making it clear which event happens first.

● Mahé wíyukha, wíčhokaŋ kiŋ úŋ.
- *Before the sun rises, the village is quiet.*

---

39. háŋtokeca — *after* — The word 'háŋtokeca' is used to indicate something that occurs later in time or sequence. It is often placed after the noun or event it describes to show that it follows another action or period. This word helps to establish a timeline or order of events in a sentence, providing clarity on when something happens relative to another event.

● Wíyukčaŋ kiŋ háŋtokeca, wíčhokaŋ hiyú kte.
- *After the meeting, they will go to the gathering.*

---

40. thípi — *home* — In Lakota, 'thípi' is used to describe something related to a home or dwelling. It can be used to convey the idea of a place where one lives or resides. The term can be applied in various contexts to indicate the concept of home, whether referring to a physical structure or the sense of belonging and comfort associated with it.

● Wíyukčaŋ kiŋ thípi waŋží él úŋpi.
- *The family lives in a home.*

---

41. táku — *great* — The word 'táku' is used to describe something of significant size, importance, or quality. It can be applied to various contexts, such as describing a person, event, or object that stands out due to its greatness. The word can be used both in literal and metaphorical senses, depending on the context.

● Táku wíyukčaŋ kiŋ lé wówašte héčha.
- *This great ceremony is beautiful.*

---

42. owáštensica — *last* — The term 'owáštensica' is used to describe something that is the final one in a sequence or series. It can refer to the last item, event, or person in a given context. This term is often used to indicate the end point of a list or order, emphasizing that there is nothing following it.

- Hé owáštensica wíčhóiye kiŋ.
- *That is the last word.*

---

43. iyéyapi kiŋ — *better* — The term 'iyéyapi kiŋ' is used to compare two or more entities, indicating that one is superior in quality, condition, or performance. It is often used in contexts where improvement or preference is being expressed. This term can be applied to various subjects, such as people, objects, or situations, to highlight their enhanced state or desirability.

- Wíyukčaŋ kiŋ iyéyapi kiŋ wíyukčaŋ héčha.
- *The new house is better than the old house.*

---

44. háŋka — *new* — The term 'háŋka' is used to describe something that is recently made, acquired, or introduced. It can be applied to objects, ideas, or experiences to indicate their recent origin or novelty. It typically precedes the noun it modifies, aligning with the standard structure in Lakota.

- Háŋka wíyukse kiŋ lé wóuŋspe kiŋ hečhí.
- *This new book is for learning.*

---

45. yeháŋni — *always* — The term 'yeháŋni' is used to describe something that occurs perpetually or without interruption. It can be applied to actions, states, or conditions that are consistent over time. This term helps to emphasize the continuity or permanence of the subject it describes.

- Wičháša yeháŋni wówaši kiŋháŋ.
- *The man always works.*

---

46. šíčala — *long* — The term 'šíčala' is used to describe objects, distances, or durations that have considerable length. It can be applied to physical dimensions, such as a long road or a tall person, as well as to time, like a long wait. The context in which it is used will determine its specific meaning, but it consistently conveys the idea of something extended or prolonged.

• Táku šičála kiŋ lé šíčala héčha.
- *This long stick is very long.*

---

47. išná — *around* — The term 'išná' is used to describe something that is surrounding or encircling an object or area. It conveys the idea of being in the vicinity or encompassing something. This term can be used in various contexts to indicate spatial relationships.

• Wíyukčaŋ waŋží išná kiŋháŋ wíčhokaŋ.
- *A tree stands around the circle.*

---

48. héčhe — *ever* — The word 'héčhe' is used to express the concept of 'ever' in a sentence. It can be used to indicate something that happens at any time or continuously. It often appears in contexts where the speaker is referring to an indefinite or ongoing period. This word helps to emphasize the timeless or perpetual nature of an action or state.

• Héčhe waŋčhíŋyaŋke šni.
- *I never see it.*

---

49. hók'ila — *old* — The term 'hók'ila' is used to describe something or someone that is old or aged. It can refer to people, animals, or objects that have been around for a long time. The context in which it is used will determine whether it conveys respect, endearment, or simply a factual description of age.

• Ťhatȟáŋka hok'íla kiŋ lé wówačhiŋyaŋ.
- *This old buffalo is wise.*

---

50. wóuŋspe kiŋ — *kind* — The word 'wóuŋspe kiŋ' translates to 'kind'. It is used to describe someone who is friendly, generous, and considerate toward others.

• He is always so wóuŋspe kiŋ to everyone he meets.
- *Thiwóuŋspe kiŋ eyápi kte lo.*

---

51. makȟóčhe — *every* — The word 'makȟóčhe' is used to indicate 'every' and is generally placed before the noun it describes.
● Makȟóčhe waníčapelo
- *Every day*

---

52. šiyé — *enough* — The word 'šiyé' is used to indicate that there is a sufficient amount or quantity of something. It implies a sense of satisfaction or completion.
● Wóglakakiyapi kičhí sičháŋtuŋ šiyé.
- *There is enough food for everyone.*

---

53. šúŋka — *today* — Used to express the concept of 'today'. It is typically used before a verb to indicate that the action is taking place on the current day.
● Wí yeló! šúŋka lé, kaŋháŋ vélkayapi.
- *Good morning! Today, I am going to work.*

---

54. opȟétȟuŋpi — *own* — The Lakota Adjective 'opȟétȟuŋpi' is used to indicate possession or ownership of something.
● Wíyakel uŋ skúyaŋ opȟétȟuŋpi kte.
- *I have my own car.*

---

55. ókac'aŋ — *same* — Used to indicate that two or more things are the same or identical in some way.
● Wíŋya ókac'aŋ napíč'uŋpi k'úŋh hékta.
- *The woman has the same dress as the girl.*

---

56. nážiŋtku — *else* — Used to indicate 'else' or 'other' in a comparison or contrast. It implies something different or additional.
● Héčha nážiŋtku kiŋ hená oíčhetu.
- *She is different from her sister.*

---

57. eháŋni tȟaŋka — *next* — The phrase 'eháŋni tȟaŋka' is u-sed to refer to something that comes after the current point in time or sequence.

● Wí yaháŋni tȟaŋka kiŋ hé aŋpétu tȟaŋka kiŋ.
- *I will see you next Friday.*

58. woíčik'iŋ — *best* — Used to describe something that is c-onsidered the best or superior.

● Nážiŋ woíčik'iŋ waníčha wóšilakel.
- *He is the best basketball player.*

59. wakáŋ — *together* — Used to express the concept of being together, united, or in close proximity.

● Wíyete na wakáŋ kiŋ, tȟokšíla ečhákupi kaga ánpo thí.
- *When we are together, nothing can stop us.*

60. éca — *thus* — Used to describe how something is done in a particular way, or in a specific manner. It is often translated as 'thus' in English.

● Wakȟáŋ éca kiŋ lená gluká.
- *He speaks thus with his parents.*

61. éthúŋ — *hence* — Used to indicate a consequence or result of a previous action or situation.

● Wíčhaša éthúŋ, khéya kiŋ ló, yámni ušpáŋ
- *The man is hungry, hence he is eating meat*

62. oyétu — *already* — Used to indicate that something has already been completed or happened.

● Toká wóihaŋ oyétu kiŋ hečá, k'a wówaso pi !
- *I have already read that book, please give me another one.*

63. wí — *most* — Used to indicate the superlative form of a quality or characteristic, meaning 'most' or 'very'. It is used to

show the highest degree of a certain attribute.
- Háŋska wí kiŋ
- *He is the most handsome.*

---

64. yuháŋ — *happy* — Used to describe someone or something that is feeling joy or pleasure.
- WíyayA yuháŋ hečéčAkin yelo.
- *My brother is happy today.*

---

65. wašík — *yet* — Used to indicate that something has not happened or been completed up to a certain point in time. It implies a sense of continuation or expectation.
- Wóihaŋble wašík kiŋ čha úŋgluhaŋpi.
- *I have not finished eating yet.*

---

66. léčhetu — *also* — Used to indicate inclusion or addition. It is used to say 'also' in a sentence.
- Wíčhaša léčhetu wašté glukápi kiŋ henápi čha
- *The man also knows how to speak Lakota*

---

67. étuŋwaŋ — *tomorrow* — Used to refer to the concept of 'tomorrow'. It indicates a future point in time that is one day after the current day.
- Wíyute lé łé étuŋwaŋ.
- *I will see you tomorrow.*

---

68. oíyok;atek — *open* — The Lakota adjective 'oíyok;atek' describes something that is not closed, accessible or not obstructed.
- Wíyuke ečíyatakhečte kiŋ, ní oíyok;atek kiŋ.
- *When you push the door, it will be open.*

---

69. héhaŋ — *ago* — Used to indicate a period of time in the past.

• Makhíze héhaŋ wašté kiŋ yeló.
- *I saw a good movie a while ago.*

---

70. hakíče — *true* — Used to describe something as being true or accurate. It is often used to confirm the correctness of statements or information.
• Anpétu kiŋ wópila po, hakíče ló li.
- *The sun is shining today, it is true.*

---

71. ayáš — *later* — Used to indicate a later time or occurrence in the future.
• Lé ayáš kiŋ kte lo, hí daŋ wakí šni.
- *I will do it later, I have something to do now.*

---

72. waštéwi — *beautiful* — Used to describe something or someone as beautiful. It is commonly used to compliment the appearance of a person, object, or scenery.
• Tokíla waštéwi kiŋ
- *The horse is beautiful*

---

73. éčhetu — *probably* — Used to indicate likelihood or probability.
• Wašté éčhetu kiŋ lé.
- *She is probably good.*

---

74. čhiyè — *young* — Used to describe something as young or youthful. It can refer to a young person or animal.
• Mála kte lo čhiyè.
- *The child is young.*

---

75. owíŋžala — *second* — Used to refer to something or someone that is the second in a sequence or order.
• Tokáhta owíŋžala tȟaópi kte.
- *He chose the second horse.*

76. kağákapi — *working* — Used to describe something that is in the process of working or being active.
- Iyápi kin kağákapi kte.
- *He is currently working.*

77. éçháŋ — *exactly* — Used to emphasize that something is done or located in a precise and accurate manner. It indicates a high level of precision or correctness.
- Wóičhoškike éçháŋ na.
- *I know exactly where it is.*

78. háŋska — *far* — Used to describe something that is located at a distance or far away from the speaker.
- Wíyuke kiŋ mázaska háŋska eyápi kiŋ he?
- *Is the bank far from here?*

79. thiŋháŋ — *inside* — Used to describe something that is positioned within a space or container.
- Wíyayawiŋ thiŋháŋ wicháȟla okóčhupi.
- *The key is inside the drawer.*

80. nážiŋ — *anyway* — Used to convey the meaning of 'anyway'. It is often used to suggest a change of topic or to continue the conversation in a different direction.
- Wí hąyą čhaŋtétakiyaye nážiŋ, héčhel.
- *We will eat dinner anyway, let's go.*

81. tȟaŋka — *dear* — Used to describe something or someone as 'dear' or 'precious'. It conveys a sense of value and importance.
- Náŋ kiŋ tȟaŋka kiŋ he? Tȟaŋkšal ye.
- *Is that your dear friend? Yes, he is dear.*

82. oíyoketekiye — *fun* — Used to describe something that is enjoyable, entertaining, or amusing.
● Wóžupi oíyoketekiye na tȟáŋka yuȟá ǧagíla.
- *The party was really fun last night.*

83. owáčekiye — *least* — Used to indicate the least or smallest amount or degree of something.
● Wíyuyake ksto owáčekiye k'ečhíčiyape.
- *He has the least amount of food.*

84. owákikiye — *quite* — Used to describe the degree or extent of something, typically emphasizing that it is quite a bit or quite a lot.
● Wíyute owákikiye yúya kiŋ hé uhaŋ wí.
- *The horse is quite fast when it runs.*

85. tȟaŋí-wašte — *important* — Used to describe something of high importance or significance.
● Hečhel tȟaŋí-wašte kiŋ. Wóuŋspe kiŋ tȟaŋí.
- *This is a very important book. The ceremony is important.*

86. tȟaŋí-tȟokéya — *anymore* — Used to express the meaning of 'anymore' in Lakota language. It indicates that a certain action or state is no longer happening or relevant.
● Wóžakila tȟaŋí-tȟokéya kiŋhadáhu.
- *I don't see her anymore.*

87. ciŋ-kiyé — *almost* — Used to indicate that something is nearly or almost a certain way.
● Wí kté kiŋ oíye ciŋkiyé.
- *I almost ate all of it.*

88. wašte — *able* — The Lakota adjective 'wašte' means 'able' or 'capable of'. It is used to describe someone or something that has the ability to do a specific action or task.

● Makh'uŋ wašte ečháŋpi kiŋ.

- *He is able to ride a horse.*

---

89. óksiŋ — *high* — Used to describe something that is physically high or tall in height.

● Čhaŋsápa óksiŋ kštó.

- *The tree is very high.*

---

90. waŋčhékhiye — *free* — Used to describe something or someone as being free or liberated.

● Hčhoka waŋčhékhiye kiŋ lenápi kta yuhá, heečha.

- *The bird flies freely over the trees.*

---

91. ziŋtkȟóški — *cool* — The word 'ziŋtkȟóški' is used to describe something as cool or cold in temperature.

● Háŋ, táku ló! Ziŋtkȟóški kiŋ rá kiŋ.

- *Wow, look at that! It's really cool over there.*

---

92. tȟokáhe — *full* — Used to describe when something is full or complete.

● Wíyute owótȟuŋ tȟokáhe.

- *The glass is full.*

---

93. okȟáte — *sometimes* — Used to describe occurrences that happen occasionally or at irregular intervals, indicating the concept of 'sometimes'.

● Okȟáte owáŋžiŋ kiŋ heháŋ tókhiyúzapi k'uŋ hé tóna okȟáte kiŋ heháŋ tókhiyúzapapi k'uŋ.

- *Sometimes I like to listen to music while I work.*

---

94. iŋyékaŋ — *outside* — Used to describe something that is located or situated on the exterior or outer side of a place or object.

- Wičhíte waste iŋyékaŋ uŋglízape yaŋkáŋpi kte.
- *The white horse is standing outside the fence.*

---

95. okháŋ — *hot* — Used to describe something as being hot in temperature.
- Mnišiŋčhaha okháŋ yelo.
- *The water is hot.*

---

96. hiŋ-néča — *funny* — The word 'hiŋ-néča' is used to describe something that is amusing or humorous.
- Níčhíŋ kiŋ lená wičhíyayapi he? Hiŋ-néča kiŋ.
- *Did you hear that story? It was funny.*

---

97. wačhíŋyeyA — *clear* — Used to describe something that is clear or transparent in appearance or meaning.
- Mni wačhíŋyeyA núŋpa ptehíŋča kiŋ héčhel.
- *The water is clear like glass.*

---

98. kičhíle — *ahead* — Used to describe something that is located in front or ahead of something else.
- Owáyawa kičhíle he? na. Kičhíle kičhíle kiwó phežúta
- *Is the store ahead? Yes. The store is ahead on the right side.*

---

99. niya-wakȟáŋ — *living* — The Lakota adjective 'niya-wakȟáŋ' means 'living' and is used to describe something that is currently alive or in a state of being alive.
- Tȟakíčhuŋpi kiŋ niyawakȟáŋ šni.
- *The flowers are living beautifully.*

---

100. ska — *white* — Used to describe something or someone as being white in color or having a white quality.
- Wan jam ska kte
- *The horse is white.*

---

101. číŋšma — *small* — Used to describe something that is small in size or stature.
- Wičháša číŋšma kiŋ čhaŋló.
- *The boy is small in height.*

102. iyótȟA — *alright* — Used to express approval or agreement. It is often used informally to signify that something is acceptable or satisfactory.
- Wíyuke kiŋ des kiyémniya, iyótȟA!
- *Let's go to the movies tonight, alright!*

103. waŋyáŋg A — *safe* — Used to describe something as being safe or secure in the Lakota language.
- Iyéčhe waŋyáŋg A haičápi.
- *The house is safe.*

104. yašpáŋ — *perfect* — Used to describe something as perfect or flawless. It conveys the idea of being without defects or shortcomings.
- Waúŋ yašpáŋ kiŋ hečelo.
- *She made a perfect dress.*

105. oyáte — *serious* — Used to describe something or someone that is considered to be serious or important.
- Ate wóihaŋke kiŋ óma iyápi kiŋ, tȟó oóyáte, kiŋ.
- *When it comes to your future, it's important to be serious about it.*

106. šá — *red* — Used to describe something as being red in color. It is commonly used to describe objects, animals, or people that are red in color.
- Iyéčha waŋ 'šá'.
- *The apple is red.*

107. mayáŋke — *perhaps* — Used to express uncertainty or possibility in Lakota.

● Wíyakśa čha éčiyapi keyá mayáŋke he?
- *Are you going to the store perhaps?*

108. ohúŋ — *back* — Used to describe something related to the back of a person or object.

● Wíčhayá yeló, hečúla ohúŋ kte.
- *Look behind you, there is a person standing.*

109. wikčémna — *human* — Used to describe something as being human or related to humans.

● Wíčháśa wikčémna kiŋ
- *The human child is playing*

110. waŋzí — *glad* — Used to express a feeling of joy or contentment.

● Iyá kiŋ waŋzí hečá
- *I am glad to see you*

111. ókskA — *cold* — Used to describe a cold temperature or feeling.

● WípazokskA kiŋ, nážiŋ kiŋ héčhetuŋpi.
- *It is cold outside, so remember to bundle up.*

112. iŋyétȟaŋka — *fast* — The word 'iŋyétȟaŋka' is used to describe something or someone that moves quickly or operates at a high speed.

● Wíkte iŋyétȟaŋka kiŋ hÉčhe.
- *The car is fast.*

113. okíyaŋ — *finally* — Used to indicate an event or action that has been anticipated or awaited, and has finally occurred.

• Wíčhaša okíyaŋ íŋyaŋhaŋ wastépi kiŋ henúŋpi.
- *The child finally finished his homework.*

114. wičháša — *sweet* — Used to describe something as sweet, in terms of taste or personality.
• Wítaŋ'yelo wičháša kiŋ lenápi kiŋ hél yelo.
- *That apple is very sweet, it is my favorite.*

115. iyówaŋšičA — *lucky* — Used to describe someone or something as fortunate or lucky in the Lakota language.
• Wíyaka hecél iyówaŋšičA kiŋ, kté lo.
- *My friend is lucky because he won the game.*

116. kiktel — *known* — Used to describe something that is known or has been recognized by someone.
• Wahčáša kiktečuŋpi kiŋ.
- *The man is known to me.*

117. waŋyáŋkapi — *quiet* — Used to describe something or someone as quiet, peaceful, or calm in the Lakota language.
• Wíyakasoke šni s'aguyapi waŋyáŋkapi.
- *The baby is sleeping quietly.*

118. okážaŋ — *somewhere* — The word 'okážaŋ' is used to refer to a place that is not specifically named or identified.
• Wíyukhla okážaŋ tuwá wíyukhla kiŋ ló.
- *I left my book somewhere.*

119. tȟótA — *longer* — Used to describe something that is longer in length or duration compared to something else.
• Wíčha tȟótA kiŋ, čhaŋlóuŋska sápa yeló.
- *The river is longer than the road.*

120. kȟóla — *straight* — Used to describe something that is in a straight line or directly across from something else.
- Iyápi kȟóla kiŋ, hečá s'áwitȟa kin - The road goes straight, then turns.
- *The road goes straight, then turns.*

---

121. wačhíŋla — *calm* — Used to describe a state of calmness or tranquility.
- Wačhíŋla na íyéčhepi.
- *She is calm now.*

---

122. waŋyáŋka — *wonderful* — Used to describe something as wonderful or amazing. It conveys a sense of awe and admiration for the subject.
- Tokátakiya waŋyáŋka kiŋ lená okíčize.
- *The beautiful sunrise is truly wonderful.*

---

123. kiní — *early* — Used to describe something that happens or is done happening at an early time.
- Wóiyokiyake kiní hécetu waŋ hé iyéčhel uŋ wí enáŋ he ómak-ayalo.
- *They woke up early this morning to go hunting.*

---

124. wàní — *quick* — Used to describe something or someone as quick or fast. It can be used to convey the idea of speed or efficiency.
- Wašté waní kiŋ lá
- *The horse is very fast*

---

125. kičhízA — *absolutely* — Used to emphasize the certainty or completeness of a statement. It conveys a strong sense of assurance or definiteness.
- Wóuŋspe kičhízA.
- *I absolutely believe.*

---

126. niá — *moving* — Used to describe something or someone that is currently in motion or moving.

● Héčhetu kiŋ niá.

- *The person is moving.*

127. tȟáŋčhiyA — *strong* — Used to describe something or - someone as strong, powerful, or sturdy.

● Wíŋyaŋ tȟáŋčhiyA kiŋ na wópila kiŋ, héčha.

- *The woman is very strong and brave.*

128. wówašte — *general* — Used to describe something as - general or all-encompassing.

● Wówašte wakȟáŋyeža kiŋ weló.

- *The general concept is good.*

129. ookíyapi — *missing* — Used to describe something that is missing or lacking.

● Tȟokáhe kiŋ ouŋžiyézapi, ookíyapi wičháȟpi kiŋ.

- *The pantry is bare, it is missing food.*

130. waŋží — *amazing* — The word 'waŋží' is used to describe something that is truly awe-inspiring or extraordinary.

● Tȟašíču waŋží kiŋ máni yelo.

- *The starry sky is truly amazing at night.*

131. tȟéčawe — *busy* — Used to describe someone who is c-onstantly occupied or engaged in activities.

● Wíyaye kiŋ tȟéčawe wašté huŋ-sni he??

- *Why are you so busy all the time??*

132. imá — *dark* — Used to describe something that is dark in color or lacking light. It can be used to describe the color of an object or the absence of light in a room.

- Wíyaka tȟáŋka imá kiŋ he?
- *Is the horse dark?*

---

133. taŋíčhA — *totally* — Used to emphasize the completeness or entirety of something. It is often used to convey the idea of totality or totalness.
- Wí tháŋka taŋíčhA kiŋ hé yelo.
- *I am totally grateful for what you did.*

---

134. wakí — *completely* — Used to express the idea of something being done or finished completely.
- Héčhaŋ wakí kiŋ, héčhaŋ kiŋ.
- *He ate completely, he ate everything.*

---

135. hówa — *instead* — Used to indicate that something is done in place of something else or in lieu of another option.
- Máza hówa híča kiŋ le hó's 'thíyute.'
- *I will eat corn instead of meat today.*

---

136. yuhá — *certainly* — Used to emphasize certainty or assurance in statements or agreements.
- Háu, yuhá kiŋ héčhel. Táku wé.
- *Yes, certainly I will come. I promise.*

---

137. to — *blue* — The Lakota adjective 'to' means 'blue' and is commonly used to describe objects or elements that have a blue color.
- Mni to yelo he.
- *The water is blue.*

---

138. wakní — *definitely* — Used to emphasize the certainty or definiteness of something. It conveys a strong sense of assurance or conviction.

● Wakní čhaŋlíčhinka kte.
- *He definitely came.*

---

139. okíčhiya — *forever* — Used to describe something that is eternal or ongoing without an end.
● Iyéčhel okíčhiya kiŋ hečá.
- *Our love will last forever.*

---

140. ičhíŋčhA — *entire* — Used to describe something as complete or whole, without any missing parts.
● Wakičhá wašíču kiŋ, héčhel uŋkíčhuŋpi.
- *The entire group arrived, except for one person.*

---

141. waŋší — *lovely* — Used to describe something that is lovely or beautiful in a positive way.
● Wí hínu waŋší kiŋ kte lo.
- *This flower is very lovely.*

---

142. hókšaŋ — *anywhere* — Used to indicate any place or location without specifying a particular one.
● Hókšaŋ na wí yeló!
- *You can sleep anywhere!*

---

143. wakáŋčhA — *simple* — Used to describe something that is simple or uncomplicated in nature.
● WakáŋčhA kiŋ gleskA yelo.
- *This task is very simple.*

---

144. mašíčA — *fair* — Used to describe something that is fair or just. It can refer to fairness in terms of color (light), justice, honesty, or equality.
● Wahčhí mašíčA kiŋ he? WíyakA waŋ sayá waúšte?
- *Is the sky fair? The clear blue sky is very fair.*

---

145. imá, waŋká — *interesting* — Used to describe something that is intriguing or captivating.
● Lakota kiŋ, imá, waŋká uŋžíŋ čhaŋte wíčhačha.
- *I find that book very interesting.*

146. máza — *short* — Used to describe something as short in length.
● Ištá mažáhuŋ čha
- *The tree is short*

147. waštélA — *normal* — Used to describe something that is considered ordinary or typical, without any special qualities or characteristics.
● WiyA waštélA kičhíčhA kiŋ héčhiya pA.
- *This is a normal day.*

148. čhíŋčhA — *personal* — Used to describe something that is personal or individual to a specific person.
● Wíčhaša čhíŋčhA kiŋ nonhí.
- *This is my personal horse.*

149. nišíčA — *proud* — Used to describe someone who has a sense of pride and confidence in themselves or their accomplishments.
● Wíčhaša nišíčA yelo.
- *The man is proud.*

150. ižáŋgúnaŋ — *english* — Used to describe anything or anyone related to the English language or culture.
● Wakhíŋ ižáŋgúnaŋ wašíču kiŋ de, wanna wíǧiča yá.
- *I learned English when I was young.*

151. uŋžíč'ipeya — *hungry* — The word 'uŋžíč'ipeya' means '-hungry'. It is used to describe the feeling of needing or wanting food.

- Mní wéiyopagiŋ uŋžíč'ipeya yeló.

- *I am very hungry for some water.*

---

152. wókisaŋ — *third* — Used to indicate the concept of 'third'. It is used to describe the placement of an item or person in a sequence, indicating that it is the third in line.

- Tokáhe kiŋ wókisaŋ tókša kiŋ yeló.

- *The third horse is brown.*

---

153. ečhíŋ — *often* — The word 'ečhíŋ' is used to describe something that happens frequently or commonly.

- Nahíŋ kiŋ he éyačhiyapi le ečhíŋ hékta.

- *I see him often when I go to town.*

---

154. wičáša — *private* — Used to describe something as private or personal. It conveys the idea of something being kept confidential or not shared with others.

- Wíčhaša kiŋ hená okíyakel šni

- *This is my private space*

---

155. wóyute — *especially* — Used to emphasize that something is particularly important or exceptional.

- Wóyute iyéčhel ečhíŋ

- *Especially good food*

---

156. čhetáŋ — *french* — Used to describe something or someone that is related to or associated with the French people or language.

- Wíyakša čhetáŋ owíčhabla čhena kiŋ láksaŋ hé.

- *I am learning French because I like it.*

---

157. zi — *green* — Used to describe anything that is green in color, such as plants, trees, or other objects.

- Wiyanzi wastelo.
- *She has a green dress.*

---

158. ičhá — *sleeping* — The word 'ičhá' is used to describe someone or something that is currently sleeping or in a state of sleep.
- Timá ithípi kiŋ, čhaŋkšiyela wašté waŋ núŋ ašlápi waŋ Thiwáhe kin hąhíŋi yelo.
- *Last night, my cat was sleeping peacefully on the bed with the family.*

---

159. šičhá — *evil* — Used to describe something or someone as evil, malevolent, or wicked.
- Tȟokáhe kiŋ šičhá na wékte kiŋ hena.
- *That person is evil and does bad things.*

---

160. kiye — *obviously* — Used to emphasize that something is obvious or evident.
- He kiye waste lo.
- *He obviously knows.*

---

161. sáŋni — *slow* — Used to describe something that is moving or taking place at a slow pace.
- 'Wíčházika owíčhazupi sáŋni kte lo.'
- *The turtle walks slow.*

---

162. tȟátAŋka — *huge* — The word 'tȟátAŋka' is used to describe something that is very large in size.
- Héčhel wašté tȟátAŋka čhúŋkíla kiŋ máza yapá.
- *The horse is very huge, it carries a heavy load.*

---

163. yuzáŋzA — *stuck* — Used to describe something that is stuck or unable to move.

● Iyé yuzáŋzA tuktépi kte lo.
- *The door is stuck and can't be opened.*

---

164. pȟó — *fat* — Used to describe someone or something as fat or thick. It is commonly used to describe the physical appearance of a person or animal.

● Iyéčhel thaŋká pȟó kiŋ weákmeyaŋke sni.
- *The bear is very fat and it is difficult to kill.*

---

165. okíkta — *suddenly* — The word 'okíkta' is used to describe something that happens quickly and unexpectedly.

● Wíčhayela tȟokáhe okíkta khloyáyapi.
- *I suddenly saw a deer.*

---

166. okíȟteŋ — *immediately* — Used to describe something that should be done without delay or instantly.

● Waúŋšila čhaštéya okíȟteŋ owíč'ičhiyapi.
- *Please come here immediately.*

---

167. iyáya — *usually* — Used to indicate something that happens or is done on a regular basis, most of the time or usually.

● Wíyayata kiŋ lená omíčiye kte
- *I usually drink coffee in the morning.*

---

168. waŋbláke — *everywhere* — Used to describe something or someone that is present in all places or locations.

● Wíyakel waŋbláke kiŋ hí.
- *The stars are everywhere in the sky.*

---

169. čhaŋtéwašte — *grand* — Used to describe something or someone as 'grand' or 'magnificent'. It conveys a sense of something being impressive or majestic.

● Wíčhaša čhaŋtéwašte hečápi kiŋ, tȟawíčhayapi hą.
- *The man built a grand house for his family.*

170. owáŋka — *final* — Used to describe something that is f-inal or ultimate. It indicates that there is nothing beyond or after that particular thing.

● He čháŋ owáŋka kižá, pté čháŋ okólakiyayelo.

- *This is the final piece of bread, I will give it to you.*

171. wašíču — *otherwise* — Used to describe something as 'otherwise' or 'different from what is expected'. It signifies a d-eviation from the norm or an alternative outcome.

● Aŋpétu wašíču kiŋ hel yelo.

- *The weather is otherwise than predicted.*

172. wóičuŋze — *innocent* — Used to describe someone or so-mething that is innocent or guiltless.

● Wóičuŋze čháŋhskawíčhakiyapi kiŋ héčhuŋ.

- *The child is innocent and pure.*

173. thípiya — *pregnant* — Used to describe a female who is pregnant.

● Iyápi thípiya kiŋ lenápi kte lo.

- *My sister is pregnant.*

174. híŋhaŋ — *further* — Used to describe something that is located at a distance or a place which is beyond the current loc-ation.

● Tȟuŋkášila kiŋ héčha híŋhaŋ óta kiŋ.

- *The holy man lives further up the hill.*

175. máku — *upstairs* — Used to describe something that is located on a higher level, typically referring to upstairs in a bui-lding.

● WíyuyA máku kičhíčapi kin.

- *The bedroom is upstairs.*

176. čhaŋté — *apart* — Used to describe something or someone that is separated or distinct from others.
- Wíčhaša čhaŋté khóye čha yúhípi kiŋ
- *The man stood apart from the group*

177. núŋpa — *twice* — The word 'núŋpa' is used to indicate something happening twice or being double in quantity.
- The dog barks núŋpa.
- *The dog barks twice.*

178. matȟó — *low* — The word 'matȟó' is used to describe something that is at a low position or level in comparison to something else.
- Mní matȟó tȟáŋka yeló.
- *The water is low in the river.*

179. taŋyáŋ — *awesome* — Used to describe something as awesome or great. It is commonly used to express admiration or wonder.
- The powwow dancers' regalia was taŋyáŋ.
- *The powwow dancers' regalia was awesome.*

180. tȟaté — *bigger* — Used to describe something larger in size or quantity than something else.
- Wíyopeya tȟaté kiŋ čhokáta.
- *The horse is bigger than the dog.*

181. owáŋ — *written* — Used to describe something that has been written down or documented.
- Háŋ'kayapi kte lo, caŋ ówiŋyan owáŋ kta yahiŋ.
- *I have to remember, my notes are written in that book.*

182. iyótake — *indeed* — Used to emphasize a statement or to confirm it as true. It is often translated as 'indeed'.

- Iyótake, wóiŋyaŋ weló!
- *Indeed, it is a beautiful day!*

---

183. olówaŋ — *empty* — The Lakota term 'olówaŋ' is used to describe something that lacks content or substance. It refers to a state of being empty or void.

- Mákȟa kičhíča olówaŋ hé.
- *The bowl is empty.*

---

184. wóyatke — *fresh* — The word 'wóyatke' is used to describe something as 'fresh' or 'new'. It is often used to refer to recently harvested or newly prepared food, as well as anything that is recently made or created.

- Čhaŋsákila wóyatke kiŋ, khéya kiŋ ahiyé.
- *The berries are fresh today, they taste good.*

---

185. wičháȟpi — *favorite* — Used to describe something as - being a favorite or preferred choice.

- Wíčhiyake'sni kiŋ kštó.
- *This is my favorite horse.*

---

186. čhékpa — *however* — Used to express contrast or contradiction in a sentence, similar to the English word 'however'. It is used to introduce a conflicting piece of information or idea.

- Wíyuke la ópȟa lúta, čhékpa waštéya kiŋ líla.
- *The water is cold, however it is refreshing to swim.*

---

187. waŋžíla — *following* — Used to describe something or - someone that is following behind or coming after something or someone else.

- Héčha waŋžíla uŋglí hékta.
- *The dog is following the cat.*

---

188. oȟníŋ — *warm* — The word 'oȟníŋ' is used to describe something that is warm in temperature.
- Aŋpetu oȟníŋ kiŋ lenápi kičížapi.
- *The day is warm and beautiful.*

189. kté — *apparently* — The word 'kté' is used to indicate that something seems or appears to be a certain way, without a definitive confirmation.
- Wíčhaša kté kiŋ hena kšní.
- *The man apparently saw the woman.*

190. iyéčheca — *asleep* — The Lakota adjective 'iyéčheca' means 'asleep'. It is used to describe someone or something that is in a state of sleep or unconsciousness.
- WíglakA wói iyéčheca.
- *The child is asleep.*

191. wakȟáŋ — *extra* — Used to describe something that is additional or extra in quantity or quality.
- Kȟaŋskála wakȟáŋ blokéya kiŋ čha tȟéya ekčiyápi.
- *There are extra books on the table.*

192. tȟíkȟa — *heavy* — Used to describe objects or things that are heavy in weight.
- Čhaŋté tȟíkȟa kiŋ le.
- *The rock is heavy.*

193. owáŋye — *famous* — Used to describe someone or something that is well-known or renowned.
- Heȟáka owáŋye kiŋ hé yelo.
- *The singer is famous and beloved.*

194. očhíŋ — *wild* — The word 'očhíŋ' is used to describe something or someone as wild in a natural or untamed sense.

- Tȟašúŋke očhíŋ kiŋ čha.
- *The horse is wild.*

---

195. woúŋspe — *excellent* — Used to describe something that is exceptional, outstanding, or of high quality.
- Wíyaye woúŋspe kiŋ hečhel.
- *You are an excellent student.*

---

196. wókiksuye — *responsible* — The word 'wókiksuye' conveys the meaning of being responsible and accountable for one's actions or duties.
- Tokatakiya wókiksuye yelo.
- *He is responsible for taking care of the children.*

---

197. tȟáŋka — *large* — Used to describe something as 'large' or 'big'. It is commonly used to denote the size or scale of an object or entity.
- Heȟáka tȟáŋka kiŋ hí.
- *The house is large.*

---

198. okíčhize — *military* — The word 'okíčhize' refers to something related to the military or military actions.
- Wíyayič'ikčaga okíčhize kiŋ hečíya tókiya!
- *The soldiers will go to the military base tomorrow!*

---

199. owówa — *common* — Used to describe something that is ordinary or widespread.
- Kté kiŋ lá owówa kiŋ hečhá.
- *That is a common occurrence.*

---

200. owóšte — *willing* — Used to describe someone who is willing or eager to do something.
- Wí na owóšte kiŋ éktu weló.
- *I am willing to help you.*

201. isnáȟna — *blind* — Used to describe someone who is blind or lacks the ability to see.
● Wíčhaša isnáȟna héčhel.
- *The man is blind.*

202. wóyuzaža — *german* — Used to describe something or someone as 'german'. It is derived from the word 'wóyuzapaya', which means 'German person'.
● Wóyuzaža iyéčhel wastépi kiŋ láǧe šni!
- *The German food that I ate was very delicious!*

203. wóyuza — *local* — Used to describe something that is specific or belonging to a particular place or area.
● He lives in the wóyuza community.
- *Owí kiwóyuza iyápi.*

204. íŋyaŋ — *main* — Used to indicate something as being the main or primary one among several others.
● Mní wíčhaša kiŋ aŋpétu kiŋ íŋyaŋ hí, yaháhdawiŋyaŋ wíčhaša kiŋ táku kiŋ.
- *Among the four boys, the youngest is the main one.*

205. wahčáŋ — *fuckin* — The word 'wahčáŋ' is used to emphasize or intensify the feeling or action described in a sentence, similar to the English word 'fuckin'.
● Iyápi kiŋ hena wahčáŋ blo zo.
- *I can't fucking believe it.*

206. katé — *knowing* — Used to describe someone who possesses knowledge or wisdom.
● Wakȟáŋ katé hecé uŋkīčhíyakapi kta!
- *The old man knows a lot about the spirits!*

207. koté — *due* — Used to indicate something that is due or owed to someone.
- Iyétu kiŋ lená waste éya ohíye kte lo.
- *I owe my friend a favor.*

208. čhúŋka — *tight* — The word 'čhúŋka' is used to describe something that is close-fitting, secure or restrained.
- Hé uŋ, čhúŋka hą́? Wóžapi wícta.
- *Hey there, is that shirt tight? It looks good.*

209. toxáŋ — *several* — Used to describe multiple items or b-eings, indicating a small number or a few.
- Iyápi kiŋ; toxáŋ čhaŋté waŋ hé
- *There are several dogs over there*

210. wahóta — *clearly* — Used to describe something that is clear or easily understood.
- Wahóta čháŋ wóiŋze yelo.
- *I can clearly see the blue sky.*

211. hokšína — *correct* — Used to indicate that something is correct or accurate. It can be used to describe a person, thing, or action that is in accordance with truth or fact.
- Hokšína wíčhayata keyá he?
- *Is that the correct answer?*

212. okíl — *hardly* — Used to express the idea of 'hardly' or 'barely'. It signifies a small amount or degree of something.
- Wíyaka okíl héčha kiŋ kte.
- *He hardly ate any food.*

213. tákȟo — *somehow* — The word 'tákȟo' is used to express the idea of 'somehow' or 'in some way'. It is often used when something is not quite clear or certain.

• Sápa tákȟo kiŋ, khéya kiŋ héčha pi.
- *The horse is somehow black and big.*

---

214. wapȟá — *natural* — Used to describe something that is in its natural state or condition, without any human interference or alteration.
• Mní wapȟá kiŋ, kaȟlá iyói yelo.
- *The water is natural and clean.*

---

215. owíŋyahȟa — *powerful* — Used to describe something or someone as powerful in the Lakota language.
• Makȟíčuŋpi owíŋyahȟa kiŋ čha ahiyá pi.
- *The storm is very powerful today.*

---

216. waŋblí — *fantastic* — Used to describe something as fantastic or wonderful.
• Lakȟóta waŋblí kiŋ lenáwitelo.
- *The Lakota language is fantastic.*

---

217. iwáŋyaŋkapi — *nearly* — Used to indicate that something is very close to being achieved or completed, but not quite there yet.
• Cante wasté kiŋ kte lo iwáŋyaŋkapi sni.
- *The good horse almost won the race.*

---

218. waóniyaŋ — *criminal* — Used to describe someone who has committed a crime or is involved in criminal activities. It is a word with negative connotations and is used to denote someone who has broken the law.
• Waníča otȟaŋ kte lo waóniyaŋ.
- *He went to jail because he is a criminal.*

---

219. owaŋ — *original* — Used to describe something as being original or first of its kind.

• Tȟaŋópi owaŋ kiŋ lená wóiyačel wóžupi.
- *The original painting is hanging on the wall.*

220. nína wašté — *super* — Used to describe something as super or excellent in quality, surpassing the standard.
• Thíyóšpaye nína wašté kiŋ čha wakhíŋyaŋ hí!
- *Our family's meal was super delicious today!*

221. owaŋyákapi — *truly* — Used to emphasize the truth or sincerity of a statement or action.
• Iyéčhe kiŋ okáyapi owaŋyákapi.
- *He speaks truly.*

222. iyúha — *nowhere* — Used to describe a location or state of being that is nowhere or nonexistent.
• Wíyakapl iyúha kiŋ - He is nowhere.
- *He nowhere is.*

223. apȟéčheyapi — *honestly* — Used to describe something that is done or said truthfully, without deceit or falsehood.
• Iháŋkye kiŋ 'apȟéčheyapi' owíčakiye kiŋčiŋ waŋyáŋ ožápi.
- *She always speaks 'honestly' and from the heart.*

224. waštélakapi — *comfortable* — Used to describe something that provides a sense of ease and relaxation, making one feel comfortable and content.
• Anpetu wastela waste kin he.
- *I feel comfortable in my home.*

225. šapȟá — *brown* — Used to describe the color brown. It can be used to refer to anything that is brown in color.
• Wímnayakel šapȟá kiŋ uŋglípi kte.
- *The horse has a brown coat.*

226. oíhħaye — *dry* — Used to describe something that lacks moisture or is not wet.
• Mní oíhħaye kiŋ
- *The land is dry*

---

227. íčhupi — *aware* — Used to describe someone who is conscious or alert in their surroundings and has a strong level of awareness.
• Wíčhupila éyá uŋ hčhó ičhíkeye.
- *He is always aware of what is happening around him.*

---

228. zíŋtka — *brilliant* — Used to describe something or someone as brilliant, shining, or outstanding.
• Thíčhiyala wí zíŋtka kiŋ hékta wóiyuha.
- *The sun is brilliant when it sets.*

---

229. wičhíŋčala — *female* — Used to describe something that is female or feminine in nature.
• Wičhíŋčala wíŋyaŋpi kte ló.
- *She is a female singer.*

---

230. wačhíŋčala — *social* — Used to describe something or someone as being related to or involving social interaction, gatherings, or relationships.
• Anpétu wasté wačhíŋčala yelo.
- *Today was a very social day.*

---

231. owášte — *handsome* — The word 'owášte' is used to describe someone or something as handsome or good looking.
• Nahan kte kičhí owášte.
- *That man is very handsome.*

---

232. owákpamni — *lately* — Used to describe something that has happened recently or lately.

- Wíyakȟa owákpamni kiŋ ahi yeló.
- *I saw him lately.*

---

233. iwáŋ — *ancient* — Used to describe something that is ancient, very old, or from a distant past.
- Héčhel waštépi kiŋ zí iwáŋ na táku yaŋ hé.
- *The rock formations on this land are very ancient.*

---

234. číkʼala — *tiny* — Used to describe something as very small or tiny in size.
- Wíčhíšičeya číkʼala kiŋ bíčhiyakel.
- *The baby bird is very tiny.*

---

235. šahíya — *spanish* — Used to describe something or someone as being Spanish. It is derived from the word 'España', which means Spain in Spanish.
- Háu mitákuyepi šahíyapi yelo.
- *I can speak Spanish.*

---

236. éčheča — *recently* — The word 'éčheča' is used to indicate that something has happened or occurred recently.
- Wíčoni éčheča khíŋ čha.
- *I saw her recently.*

---

237. owá — *wet* — Used to describe something that is wet or damp.
- Mní owá kiŋ lenáya, yápa kontrolápi.
- *The ground is wet, so be careful.*

---

238. wakáb — *kinda* — Used to convey a sense of something being 'kinda' or 'somewhat' a certain way, indicating a level of uncertainty or approximation.
- Ištáwaxošni wakáb ištá.
- *The food is kinda hot.*

239. zí — *bright* — Used to describe something bright or shining.

● Wí zí kto

- *The star is bright*

240. owíċakiya — *soft* — The word 'owíċakiya' is used to describe something that is soft in texture or feel.

● Ní kiŋ jan ye owíċakiya.

- *This blanket is very soft.*

241. čhó — *harder* — Used to indicate a comparative degree of hardness, meaning 'harder' in English.

● WíyukA hípi čhó kA

- *The rock is harder than the wood*

242. žuŋkála — *ill* — Used to describe someone who is feeling unwell or sick.

● Háŋ mitȟáwaži wačhíŋni yelo. Žuŋkála kiŋ.

- *I cannot go to work today. I am feeling ill.*

243. ošni — *hidden* — Used to describe something that is concealed or not easily seen.

● Hoksila wan ošni he unkacipi kta!

- *The boy has hidden the candy!*

244. miye — *personally* — Used to indicate something that is personally done or experienced by an individual.

● Wakisuye miye kte lo.

- *I did it personally.*

245. ošnaye — *sudden* — Used to describe something that happens quickly or unexpectedly, like a sudden change in weather or a sudden noise.

● Wana ośnaye tȟaŋka kiŋ avec'iyapi.
- *The sudden thunder scared the children.*

---

246. léčhaŋ — *barely* — Used to indicate that something is b-arely happening or barely present.
● Wíčhuŋkoyakapi kiŋ léčhaŋ khíyeciya.
- *I can barely see the stars.*

---

247. wačhíŋyAśi — *exciting* — Used to describe something tha-t is thrilling or stimulating.
● TokátA wačhíŋyAśi kičhíča.
- *The movie is exciting.*

---

248. wanáǧi — *downstairs* — Used to describe something that is located downstairs or on a lower level.
● Wanáǧi wicíkičiyake kiŋ iyápi kta.
- *The bedroom is downstairs in the house.*

---

249. oláȟiŋ — *obvious* — Used to describe something that is easily noticed or understood without the need for explanation.
● Wíyakel óláȟiŋ kiŋ čha.
- *The answer is obvious.*

---

250. wóŋyaŋg wačhíŋyuhápi — *professional* — The word 'wóŋ-yaŋg wačhíŋyuhápi' means 'professional'. It describes someone who is skilled and experienced in a certain area of expertise.
● Wičhíyapi kiŋ uŋkáŋpi yé wóŋyaŋg wačhíŋyuhápi kiŋ hé ǧdé tókahe.
- *He is a professional chef and makes delicious food.*

---

251. opáwŋaŋ — *foreign* — Used to describe something or -someone as foreign or outside of one's own cultural group.
● Héčhel kiŋ is'ópi kiŋ, opáwŋaŋ kiŋ wíyakapéya.
- *When I visited the city, everything felt foreign.*

252. toháŋča — *romantic* — Used to describe something related to romance or romantic emotions.
- Wíyakel rómakča toháŋča kiŋ léčhel yužápi.
- *They had a very romantic evening together.*

253. oškáŋ — *grown* — Used to describe something that has reached maturity or has fully developed, typically referring to plants or animals.
- Wíčhuȟake oškáŋ tȟáŋka waštépi kiŋ lé.
- *The corn has grown very tall this year.*

254. iyÁ — *familiar* — The Lakota adjective 'iyá' is used to describe something or someone that is familiar or known to the speaker.
- Tokáh iyá kiŋ čha wokáŋ.
- *That person is very familiar to me.*

255. akáŋl — *higher* — Used to describe something that is physically positioned at a higher level than something else.
- Wíčhayela okíyo eyá àkáŋl na hena uŋskáyaya.
- *The bird is perched higher than the tree.*

256. waúŋ šnáśe — *likely* — Used to indicate a high probability or likelihood of something happening or being true.
- Wayúŋ šnáśe kiŋ hétan wowášakel.
- *It is likely that it will rain tomorrow.*

257. toší — *younger* — Used to indicate that something or someone is younger in comparison to something or someone else.
- Háŋpa toší wéwičhayapi kte he
- *He is teaching the younger students.*

258. opáčuŋ — *indistinct* — The term 'opáčuŋ' is used to describe something that is unclear or difficult to perceive clearly.
• Tokáhe kiŋ opáčuŋ he.
- *The rock is indistinct.*

---

259. oyáŋkA — *carefully* — The word 'oyáŋkA' is used to describe the action of being careful or cautious in a situation. It is often used to emphasize the importance of paying attention to detail and avoiding mistakes.
• Wíyukšite kiŋ ómniciye čiyúzapi waúŋ okíčiye oyáŋkA héčhu.
- *He handled the delicate glassware carefully to avoid breaking it.*

---

260. sapsáčA — *sexy* — Used to describe someone or something as sexy or attractive.
• Wíčhaša sapsáčA čhiyúzA.
- *The man is very sexy.*

---

261. tȟaŋkál — *delicious* — Used to describe something as delicious or tasty. It is commonly used when referring to food or drinks that are enjoyable to eat.
• Wíčhípi wasté tȟaŋkál kštó.
- *This soup is very delicious.*

---

262. oȟáŋke — *tall* — Used to describe something or someone that is tall in height.
• Wíyakča oȟáŋke uŋglúka yelo.
- *The tree is tall.*

---

263. oȟáŋ — *sexual* — Used to describe something related to sexual activities or attributes.
• Wíyuhila oȟáŋ kiŋ gíla tókáhe.
- *He has a sexual relationship with that woman.*

---

264. waúŋ — *particular* — Used to emphasize a specific or particular aspect of something.

● Wíčha waúŋ tȟáŋka kiŋ čha.

- *I want a particular book.*

---

265. ziŋtkála — *golden* — Used to describe something that is golden in color or has qualities similar to gold.

● Héčhel waŋziŋtkála kiŋ hí kiŋ čha itȟáŋčhaŋ!

- *The sun shines so brightly and looks golden!*

---

266. wačhíŋye — *positive* — The Lakota adjective 'wačhíŋye' means 'positive' and is used to describe something that is good, beneficial, or in favor.

● Akesniyake wasté wačhíŋye kiŋ.

- *The food was really good.*

---

267. toháŋ kiŋ — *wherever* — Used to indicate a location that is unspecified or unknown, similar to the English word 'wherever'. It is used to express a general sense of place without specifying a particular location.

● Wí taŋí yelo toháŋ kiŋ.

- *I will find you wherever you are.*

---

268. waŋná — *regular* — Used to describe something as regular or normal in the Lakota language. It is often used to indicate consistency or conformity to a standard.

● Šni kiŋ, waŋná hečhu!

- *Eat well, be regular!*

---

269. stéya — *clever* — Used to describe someone who is quick-witted and sharp-minded, possessing cleverness and intelligence.

● Haŋ mitákuye othíša stéya kiŋ uŋkokiyakaye.

- *My brother is very clever.*

---

270. snuhe — *pure* — Used to describe something that is pure or uncontaminated.
- Wakan snuhe ki le, hena uniyeka.
- *The water is pure and clean.*

---

271. piyá — *healthy* — The Lakota adjective 'piyá' means healthy and is used to describe a person or thing that is physically fit and well-being.
- Nážiŋ kiŋ he? Piyá né.
- *How are you feeling? I am healthy.*

---

272. toháŋ pi — *aside* — The phrase 'toháŋ pi' is used to indicate that something is placed or located away from a central point or focus.
- Iyášiŋkiŋ toháŋ pi kté iyéčhe kiŋlápi.
- *The book is placed aside on the table.*

---

273. oȟáte — *physical* — Used to describe something that is related to the physical body or material world.
- Wíla wóuŋspe oȟáte kiŋ
- *She has a strong physical body*

---

274. waŋní — *awake* — Used to describe someone or something that is awake or alert.
- Š'úŋkawakíčiŋ waŋní yelo.
- *The dog is awake.*

---

275. ȟečháŋ — *firm* — The word 'ȟečháŋ' means firm or strong, indicating solid stability or resistance to pressure or change.
- Wíčhaša owíyospaya kiŋ ȟečháŋ yeló.
- *The man's handshake is firm.*

---

276. okšíčha — *central* — Used to describe something that is in the middle or central position within a specific context.

- Héčhetu igíya okšíčha keyá čha
- *The central star is very bright*

---

277. tȟo — *prime* — The Lakota Adjective 'tȟo' is used to describe something as being at its prime or optimal state.
- Wíyohpi tȟo.
- *The horse is prime.*

---

278. čhaŋté čhoŋ — *capable* — The phrase 'čhaŋté čhoŋ' describes someone or something as being able or capable of performing a task or action.
- Wóphila čhaŋté čhoŋ kiŋ waste héčhe.
- *I am capable of speaking Lakota language.*

---

279. waȟpé — *decent* — Used to describe something as being decent or satisfactory. It can be used to convey the idea of something being of good quality or standard.
- Wíyaká šni hé waȟpé.
- *This food is decent.*

---

280. waúŋspe kiŋháŋ — *modern* — Used to refer to something that is modern or contemporary in nature.
- Hečíya waúŋspe kiŋháŋ uȟáŋžičeye.
- *He drives a modern car.*

---

281. wóksape — *grateful* — The Lakota adjective 'wóksape' describes a feeling of gratitude or being thankful.
- Wóksape kiŋ né su.
- *I am grateful for you.*

---

282. wačhiŋyuhápi — *extremely* — Used to convey the meaning of 'extremely' or 'very'. It adds emphasis to the adjective it is describing, indicating a high degree of the quality.

- Iyápi kiŋ wačhiŋyuhápi t'áku kiŋ ekhéya.
- *She is extremely intelligent.*

---

283. ičháŋčha — *curious* — Used to describe someone who is curious and eager to learn or know more about something.
- Wíyakastan ičháŋčha kiŋ lábla yelo.
- *The child is curious about the new book.*

---

284. ošnayaŋ — *someday* — Used to refer to an unspecified point in the future, similar to the English word 'someday'. It is often used to express hope or anticipation for something that may happen in the future.
- Wahč�pi ošnayaŋ tawa kte lo!
- *I will visit you someday!*

---

285. ošmá — *silent* — Used to describe something or someone that is silent, quiet, or not making any sound.
- Hé iyápi ošmá.
- *The child is silent.*

---

286. waúŋspe — *properly* — Used to describe something done correctly or in a suitable manner.
- Ni waúŋspe tȟawápi kiŋ hena.
- *I cooked the food properly.*

---

287. ksá — *wise* — The Lakota adjective 'ksá' means 'wise' and is used to describe someone who shows good judgment and understanding.
- Makháša wóčheksa ognákičhupi.
- *The elder woman is very wise.*

---

288. waúŋ ye — *mostly* — Used to describe something that is mostly or predominantly a certain way.

- Wíčhákȟe šni héčhešničiyag waúŋ ye.
- *The sky is mostly blue.*

---

289. amášoŋ — *deeply* — Used to describe the depth of a feeling, emotion, or experience. It conveys a sense of intensity and profoundness.
- Wíyaka čháŋ amášoŋ kiŋ hečáktuya.
- *I love you deeply.*

---

290. wáŋlake — *directly* — Used to describe something that is happening immediately or directly without any delays or interruptions.
- Wáŋlake kiŋ hču wóihaŋ.
- *He spoke to me directly.*

---

291. owále — *popular* — Used to describe something that is well-liked or commonly favored by people.
- Mní owále wóišteyan kičhízapi.
- *The popular movie is showing tonight.*

---

292. tokéšni — *thereby* — The Lakota adjective 'tokéšni' is used to indicate a consequence or result of a previous action or situation.
- WíčhayA šni ThiyóšpayA tokéšni kte lo.
- *He went to school and thereby learned there.*

---

293. aokȟáþe — *separate* — The word 'aokȟáþe' is used to describe when things or people are apart or not connected.
- Háŋ aokȟáþe kiŋ eyápi.
- *The two houses are separate.*

---

294. wakȟéčha — *precious* — Used to describe something that is considered valuable, cherished, or precious.

- Máza wakȟéčha kiŋ lená itókab wóihaŋži.
- *This bracelet is so precious to me.*

295. ítkala — *spoken* — The Lakota adjective 'ítkala' means '-spoken' and is used to describe something that has been orally communicated or expressed.
- Wówašíču waŋ 'ítkala kštó' čhiŋ.
- *The teacher gave a spoken exam.*

296. wahíŋyaŋ — *merry* — Used to describe someone or something as being cheerful, happy, and full of joy.
- Wíyokiyapi kiŋ ní toksa ksto, wahíŋyaŋ kečíyapi.
- *When he tells a story, he is very merry.*

297. toknA — *direct* — Used to describe something as direct or straightforward.
- Háŋ, makȟása blatá 'toknA' ecín kiŋ he wašté!.
- *Yes, I prefer to take the most direct route when traveling!*

298. tȟaŋní — *wide* — The Lakota adjective 'tȟaŋní' means 'wide' and is used to describe something that has a large distance from side to side. It can be used to describe physical objects or abstract concepts.
- Héčha tȟaŋní kiŋ, teópi ožúŋyaŋpi kta hétuŋpi kte.
- *The road is wide and easy to drive on.*

299. ŏitke — *rare* — Used to describe something that is rare or uncommon.
- Tokatakiya kiŋ ŏitke t'okicijipi kte lo.
- *I have a rare book.*

300. wačhiŋyuhá — *successful* — Used to describe someone or something that has achieved a goal or met a desired outcome.

- Nážiŋ kiŋ wačhiŋyuhá kiŋ he?
- *Did you have a successful day?*

---

301. opáȟíŋ — *alien* — Used to describe something or someone that is foreign or unfamiliar.
- Háŋska wíčhašta waŋ héčha opáȟíŋ kte.
- *The technology he is using is alien to me.*

---

302. okȟí — *senior* — Used to describe someone who is older or senior in age or position.
- Wičháša okȟí kiŋ heéčhata piyápi.
- *The elder man is very wise.*

---

303. itȟáŋka — *sometime* — Used to describe a vague or unspecified point in time, meaning 'sometime'. It does not provide a specific time frame but rather a general indication of when something may happen.
- Was'uŋ wowápi waŋ 'itȟáŋka' yawáŋpi yuŋ háŋ.
- *I will go visit my grandmother 'sometime' this week.*

---

304. aȟakyápi — *chosen* — Used to describe something or someone that has been selected or preferred over others.
- Wíčhaŋčaŋ aȟakyápi kiŋ híčiyakel he?
- *Why did you choose that particular book?*

---

305. stȟáŋkA — *sharp* — The word 'stȟáŋkA' is used to describe something that has a sharp or pointed edge or tip.
- Iyápi kiŋ ahiŋ stȟáŋkA kte.
- *The knife has a sharp edge.*

---

306. okȟá — *leading* — Used to describe something or someone that is seen as leading or being in charge.
- Wíyakȟa wašté okȟa.
- *The good chief is leading.*

307. soksáŋ — *similar* — Used to describe things that are similar or alike in some way.
• Wí sahá cik'ala soksáŋ.
- *We have similar hair.*

308. itáŋčhaŋyaŋ — *international* — Used to describe something that is pertaining to or involving multiple countries or nations.
• Tȟáŋka Wašté is an itáŋčhaŋyaŋ organization promoting global peace and unity.
- *Tȟáŋka Wašté wóiyawapi kte lo international osícehéča na náǧnáǧ yeko.*

309. théȟówaŋka — *federal* — Used to describe something that pertains to the federal government or federal matters.
• Héčhetu wóokam wíyaka kičhíča héhaŋyépi hí. Théȟówaŋka háŋhe héčhetu kiŋ lénu ečíyapi kiŋ ló.
- *The federal government passed a new law yesterday. The federal official will visit our reservation tomorrow.*

310. síću — *alert* — Used to describe someone who is alert or attentive, being aware of their surroundings and ready to react quickly.
• Wí máni yeló síću.
- *The horse is always alert.*

311. ómakiyA — *emotional* — Used to describe something or someone that is emotional or feeling deeply. It can refer to feelings such as sadness, happiness, anger, or excitement.
• Waníyetu Kiŋ ló.ómakayo kta
- *Winter is very emotional.*

312. zítka — *pink* — Used to describe the color pink.
• Taku zítka sú ačháŋpi kiŋ zaŋžiŋla wóškalaka.
- *I like to wear a pink dress to the party.*

313. atá — *terrific* — Used to describe something as terrific or great. It is often used to express admiration or praise.
- Háŋ, éčhopi wasté atá!
- *Wow, that painting is terrific!*

314. wičháȟičA — *highly* — Used to emphasize the degree of something being high or elevated.
- Wíčhiyapi hečel suzí wičháȟičA ečháŋ
- *The mountain peak is highly elevated and beautiful*

315. ðáŋ — *previously* — Used to indicate that something has happened or existed in the past, before the current moment.
- Wíyayela óǧe: miye yúŋ ná ómažapi úñ ðáŋ.
- *She told me that she had already eaten.*

316. aúŋspe — *entirely* — Used to describe something that is whole or complete, without any parts missing.
- Aníčetu kiŋ, sunka wakan ečhaŋšiča aúŋspe.
- *The sacred dog dance is entirely beautiful.*

317. šéyA — *solid* — The word 'šéyA' is used to describe something that is solid, firmly set, or stable.
- WíyA kiŋ néwóčhuŋ šéyA yelú.
- *The house is built on solid ground.*

318. wóuŋspekte — *useful* — The Lakota adjective 'wóuŋspekte' means 'useful' and is used to describe something that is helpful or serves a useful purpose.
- Wóuŋspekte kiŋ čha wóihaŋke čhaŋpšičayapi kte lo.
- *This tool is very useful for fixing the fence.*

319. haŋká — *latest* — Used to describe something as the most recent or latest in time or order.

- Mniká hca hehánka kiŋ
- *He is wearing the latest clothes*

320. anúŋpe — *daily* — Used to describe something that occurs on a daily basis.
- Owáŋ anúŋpe kiŋ hena kte ló.
- *I drink water daily.*

321. wóglake — *shy* — Used to describe someone who is shy or bashful in Lakota language.
- Wóglake čhaŋté kiŋ héčha kiŋ ló!
- *The shy girl does not want to speak!*

322. okȟátA — *bound* — Used to describe something that is bound or tied together.
- Iyápi kiŋ okȟátA yeló.
- *The book is bound.*

323. wóglake šni — *unique* — Used to describe something as unique or one-of-a-kind. It implies that the thing being described is unlike anything else.
- Wóglake šni čhiyúzapi kiŋ hená ečéla waste t'háŋ.
- *This artwork is truly unique and beautiful.*

324. wówakȟe — *potential* — Used to describe something that has the ability or capacity to become something else.
- Háŋ mitákuye oúŋkča wówakȟe.
- *All living beings have the potential.*

325. itztáŋ — *sensitive* — Used to describe someone who is sensitive, particularly in terms of emotions or feelings.
- Wíłuŋyaŋ itztáŋ kiŋ hé eyápič'iyéč'api.
- *She is very sensitive when it comes to expressing her emotions.*

326. iȟúŋšičA — *mobile* — Used to describe something that is able to move or be easily transported.
- Waúŋšila ičíyapi kiŋ hé ȟčháŋ iȟúŋšiča yamní.
- *The mobile phone is easy to carry.*

327. oíyokiphiye — *joint* — Used to describe something that is joint or connected.
- Mazí oíyokiphiye kiŋ de Očhéthi Šakówiŋ.
- *The Lakota people are joint with the Earth.*

328. išnála — *steady* — Used to describe something that is stable, constant, or not easily moved. It implies a sense of reliability or consistency.
- Wóihaŋšiča išnála kiŋ héčhakhiŋ yeló.
- *The old dog is steady when it walks.*

329. wahákȟA — *mighty* — Used to describe something or someone as powerful or strong. It conveys the idea of mightiness or greatness.
- WahákȟA wíyakA po.
- *The bear is mighty.*

330. tókȟa — *anytime* — Used to describe something that can happen at any time or is available at all times.
- I will be available to help you anytime.
- *Iyokȟählen'opapi kta hé.*

331. wičhóiye — *online* — The Lakota adjective 'wičhóiye' translates to 'online'. It is used to describe something that is connected to the internet or available on the internet.
- Wíčhóiye takúŋpi kte ló.
- *I am shopping online.*

332. tȟaŋkÁ — *massive* — Used to describe something that is very large, huge, or massive in size.
- Wí wašté tȟaŋká kiŋ
- *The buffalo is massive*

---

333. wičháŋčhalu — *noble* — The Lakota adjective 'wičháŋčhalu' means 'noble' and is used to describe someone or something of distinguished character or high moral qualities. It is often used to express respect or admiration for a person's behavior or actions.
- Tokahe wičháŋčhalu he ya!
- *The man is noble!*

---

334. wóoyawaŋ — *civil* — The term 'w hoyawa hg' is used to describe something or someone as civil, demonstrating polite and respectful behavior.
- Wóoyawaŋ na kȟaŋšíč'iyapi kte lo.
- *He is being civil during the meeting.*

---

335. ziŋtkáluta — *orange* — Used to describe the color orange.
- Héčanktu kiŋziŋtkáluta ečél waŋyél kiŋži wašté
- *The sunset looks beautiful with its orange hue*

---

336. čhwayáya — *hopefully* — Used to express hope or wish for a desired outcome.
- Šni héčhe ašní čhwayáya kiŋ uŋglúkin.
- *I hope the weather will be nice tomorrow.*

---

337. nakúŋ — *practically* — Used to express the idea of something being close to or almost a certain quality or state.
- 'Éyahe nakúŋ wóuŋspe kiŋ, hápi kiŋ héčha.'
- *He is practically fluent in English, he just needs practice.*

---

338. hačhá — *specific* — Used to describe something that is specific or particular.

• Tokáhe kiŋ hi, hačhá wóiye.

- *This horse is specific.*

---

339. wadé — *everyday* — Used to describe something that o-ccurs on a daily basis or is common.

• Wiyópeya hé opȟéčha kiŋ he wadé.

- *I see my friend every day.*

---

340. psíč — *mysterious* — Used to describe something that is difficult to understand or explain, often leaving people feeling puzzled or intrigued.

• Wíčhaša šni héčha kiŋ jí psíč.

- *The strange man has a mysterious look.*

---

341. waštéčha — *attractive* — Used to describe something or someone as attractive or beautiful.

• Háŋ waštéčha kiŋ héčhel.

- *That flower is very attractive.*

---

342. oíkčakiyA — *heavily* — Used to describe something that has a great amount of weight or density, indicating that it is h-eavy.

• Wíyowaste oíkčakiyA yelo.

- *The bag is heavily filled.*

---

343. ičháŋ — *touching* — Used to describe something or som-eone who is physically touching something else.

• Wašíču kiŋ lená 'ičháŋ' tókáhte kiŋ.

- *The white person is touching the tree.*

---

344. waníć — *plain* — Used to describe something as plain or simple in appearance or design.

- Makhíči kiŋ níyawápi waníć yelo.
- *I prefer plain blankets.*

345. tȟá, — *particularly* — The Lakota adjective 'tȟá' is used to emphasize or single out a particular quality or characteristic of something.
- Wí kiŋ he éyá tȟá kiŋ
- *That horse is particularly fast*

346. wenáȟčháŋla — *classic* — Used to describe something as classic, timeless, or traditional.
- Háŋska wenáȟčháŋla kiŋ he
- *This song is a classic*

347. wóowacákiȟi — *financial* — Used to describe something related to finances or money.
- Wówačekiȟi kiŋ le čhaŋtéšičeya hčhaŋl hé úŋsíøni.
- *I need financial assistance to buy a new car.*

348. sápe — *frankly* — Used to express honesty and directness in speech, similar to the English word 'frankly'. It signals that the speaker is being straightforward and candid in their communication.
- Sápe, owáye kiŋyáŋ he? - Sápe, Iyápi he? - Sápe, yuháŋ Iyápi. - Sápe, tȟaŋka iyóka.
- *Frankly, what do you want? - Frankly, do you know? - Frankly, I don't know. - Frankly, it's big.*

349. waštékilA — *generous* — Used to describe someone who freely gives or shares without expecting anything in return. It conveys the idea of being generous and kind.
- WaštékilA kičhiyA wóiye.
- *He is a generous person.*

350. wóslolye — *religious* — Used to describe something that is related to or connected with religion or spirituality.
● Wóslolye wakan owasin.
- *The sacred pipe is religious.*

351. hačhá oyúsaza — *dramatic* — The Lakota adjective 'hačhá oyúsaza' is used to describe something as dramatic or striking, usually in a theatrical or emotional sense.
● Wíičhaša tókša hačhá oyúsaza kiŋ hí, épelo.
- *The play last night was very dramatic and emotional.*

352. otȟaŋi — *valuable* — The Lakota Adjective 'otȟaŋi' is used to describe something that is considered valuable or precious.
● Hékta óyakča otȟaŋi kičhí okíhičiyapi.
- *My grandmother gave me a valuable gift.*

353. waštéčake — *pleasant* — Used to describe something that is pleasant or enjoyable.
● Nonhparí aóunkičayuzapi kin hé waštéčake.
- *I had a pleasant time at the park.*

354. waŋži — *distant* — Used to describe something that is far away in space or time, or to convey a sense of emotional distance.
● Tȟašúŋke waŋži
- *The house is far away*

355. wásteya — *someplace* — Used to indicate a general location or unspecified place in the Lakota language.
● Wásteya wayážiŋ kte éyahe kiŋ he?
- *Did you leave something someplace around here?*

356. oówaŋyaŋk — *western* — Used to describe something that is related to or located in the western direction.

- Oówaŋyaŋk he unkîyapi kte ló.
- *They live to the west of us.*

---

357. ištanála — *gentle* — Used to describe something that is gentle in nature, soft, or mild.
- Wíčhašíčila kiŋ, ištanála kiŋ héčhel.
- *The horse is strong, but gentle as well.*

---

358. waŋnáke — *forth* — Used to describe something that is moving forward or progressing in a certain direction.
- Hečéšta waŋnáke kiŋ hÉtaŋhaŋpi kin
- *The horse is moving forth towards the mountain*

---

359. oákaŋke — *officially* — Used to indicate that something is done in an official or formal manner. It is often used to describe actions or events that have been officially recognized or approved.
- Tokála oákaŋke kiŋ hčíǧe tȟáŋka tȟáŋka čhokáta kiŋ yúȟpe lo.
- *The government officially announced the new policy.*

---

360. owályaŋpi — *basic* — Used to describe something as basic, simple, or fundamental.
- Aíče kiŋ Cokasíčiya wowályaŋpi kiŋ hečiyapi.
- *This recipe is very basic and easy.*

---

361. škáŋškáŋ — *incredibly* — Used to emphasize the intensity or extreme nature of a quality or action.
- Wičháškaŋškaŋ weló.
- *He runs incredibly fast.*

---

362. wičhimna — *greek* — Used to describe something or - someone as Greek. It indicates a connection to Greek culture, language, or people.

• He iyuha wicasa yelo: wičhimna yamni uŋglaksape.
- *That man is Greek: he speaks Greek fluently.*

---

363. šápe — *gray* — Used to describe the color gray. It can be used to describe objects, animals, or people that are gray in color.
• Wítaša kiŋ hoksilí okáhe šápe nažíŋ.
- *The wolf's fur is a beautiful shade of gray.*

---

364. otȟúŋwaŋ — *underground* — Used to describe something that is underground or beneath the surface of the Earth.
• Makhíčaga owáyawa otȟúŋwaŋ napé tȟawíčhupi kte.
- *The rabbit dug a hole underground to live in.*

---

365. wówapi wóyakapi — *downtown* — Used to describe a location that is in or relating to downtown in an urban area.
• Mní wóyakapi tȟáŋka yé.
- *I live in downtown Minneapolis.*

---

366. wóiyokiyA — *reasonable* — The word 'wóiyokiyA' is used to describe something that is logical, sensible, or fair.
• Lowan pi kte he? WóiyokiyA.
- *Did you sell the car? That's reasonable.*

---

367. owályaŋkapi — *equal* — Used to describe something that is equal in size, shape, quantity, or importance.
• Hečhiya owályaŋkapi čhíŋya wašté kiŋ tȟaŋháŋ tȟawápi.
- *They have equal amount of good qualities and bad qualities.*

---

368. iyópta — *nearby* — Used to describe something that is near or close by.
• Wíyakčeka kičhiyakel iyópta wíyayake.
- *The store is nearby our house.*

---

369. waštékatA — *intelligent* — Used to describe someone who is intelligent, smart, or wise.
● Hé waštékatA yAglAgA.
- *He is very intelligent.*

370. waštéčaka — *favourite* — Used to describe something or someone that is a favorite or preferred choice.
● WíyakA iyéčakiya waštéčaka kiŋ ?
- *What is your favorite color?*

371. išniya — *merely* — Used to indicate that something is done only or solely, emphasizing the simplicity or smallness of the action.
● Waúŋšila išniya yo.
- *He merely sat down.*

372. íyašiŋ — *smooth* — Used to describe something that has a smooth surface or texture.
● Wakíčhoka íyašiŋ kiŋ hé tuwéčhuŋpi
- *The stone is smooth when you touch it.*

373. š'íŋ — *precisely* — Used to convey the meaning of 'precisely' or 'exactly' in English. It is a word that emphasizes accuracy or correctness in a statement or action.
● Waníyetu š'íŋ ečhíčhaŋpi.
- *It is precisely winter now.*

374. okȟóȟi — *confident* — The word 'okȟóȟi' is used to describe someone who is self-assured and has faith in their abilities.
● Wíyahpe kiŋ ómakȟa okȟóȟi yelo.
- *He is very confident in his work.*

375. waštéwaŋ — *minor* — Used to describe something or someone as being minor, meaning it is small or of lesser importance.

• Waštéwaŋ ktelo kiŋ de tawečhaŋ pi.
- *The minor child is playing there.*

---

376. éčhA — *worthy* — The word 'éčhA' is used to signify something or someone that is deserving of respect or consideration, usually due to positive qualities or actions.
• Naháŋ éčhA kiŋ lená wóphila na akháŋštaya.
- *That person is worthy of our trust and respect.*

---

377. wíŋyaŋkiyA — *extreme* — Used to describe something that is extremely intense, severe or beyond the normal range.
• Hešíŋ šni, wíŋyaŋkiyA lo.
- *Today is extremely hot.*

---

378. owáŋskeya — *technically* — The word 'owáŋskeya' is used to convey the idea of something being done in a technically accurate or precise manner.
• Iyéčhiŋkiŋ chíŋta owáŋskeya héčha kta líla.
- *He always follows the rules technically.*

---

379. waštéyA — *scientific* — The word 'waštéyA' is used to describe something as scientific or related to science.
• Mní is a waštéyA way of studying the world.
- *Water is a scientific way of studying the world.*

---

380. hapíŋ — *previous* — Used to describe something that occurred or existed before the current time or situation.
• Wičháša hapíŋ waúŋšila kiŋ héčha.
- *The man was previously a warrior.*

---

381. waštéȟčA — *absolute* — Used to describe something as absolute or complete, emphasizing the highest level of quality or certainty.

- Háŋ waštéȟčA kiŋ
- *This is absolutely beautiful.*

---

382. waštéwóoki — *divine* — Used to describe something as divine or sacred, indicating a sense of holiness or reverence.
- Wakan Tanka okihi waštéwóoki ksto.
- *The Great Spirit is truly divine.*

---

383. waštéčhake — *fascinating* — Used to describe something that is captivating or intriguing.
- Héčhel waštéčhake lo.
- *That book is fascinating.*

---

384. waštá — *commercial* — Used to describe something that is related to commerce, business, or buying and selling goods or services.
- Wašté wíyan po! Tȟašúŋke kiŋ.
- *Buy that good woman! Give medicine to her.*

---

385. waštéyapi — *thirsty* — Used to describe the feeling of needing to drink water or other liquid because of dehydration.
- Wíyeya waštéyapi kiŋ hí.
- *I am feeling thirsty right now.*

---

386. wašték — *jumping* — Used to describe something or someone that is jumping or leaping.
- Wíyakel waštékiye kiŋ yuhápi.
- *The rabbit is jumping high.*

---

387. waštékiya — *typical* — Used to describe something as typical or usual.
- Héčhel kiŋ waštékiya kiŋ heápi kte.
- *This is a typical way of doing things.*

---

388. wíówaŋ — *fabulous* — Used to describe something as fabulous or fantastic.
- Tokáta ókiya kiŋ hékta wíówaŋ.
- *The horse race was absolutely fabulous.*

---

389. waštéki — *eternal* — Used to describe something that is eternal or everlasting.
- Wíyowapi kiŋ lená 'waštéki' yelo.
- *The love between us is eternal.*

---

390. waštéya — *moral* — The word 'waštéya' is used to describe something that is considered morally good or virtuous according to Lakota culture.
- Wíyakalapi waštéya kiŋ hektaŋ he.
- *He always makes morally good decisions.*

---

391. waštéčhapi — *sandy* — Used to describe something as 'sandy', referring to an area or material that is composed of or covered in sand.
- Makhá ȟtá waštéčhapi kiŋ uŋgluniyéla.
- *I like to walk on the sandy beach.*

---

392. waštélawapi — *peaceful* — Used to describe something or someone as peaceful or calm.
- Wíyakwecikta waštélawapi yelo.
- *The lake is very peaceful today.*

---

393. štanžaŋ — *internal* — Used to describe something that is located or situated on the inside or within.
- Wíyakel štanžaŋ kiŋ ló ȟčhékta pi kta.
- *The feelings are internal and already done.*

---

394. oláŋpa — *southern* — Used to describe something or someone that is located or connected to the southern direction.

- Wíŋkte kiŋ zin ku óláŋpa hčhéčhu.
- *The deer is grazing in the southern field.*

395. waštákečha — *nicely* — Used to describe something as being done well or nicely.
- Wíchíyela waštákečha kiŋ lená yélo.
- *You speak nicely.*

396. waštékáŋča — *random* — Used to describe something that is random or without a specific pattern or order.
- Iháŋže waštékáŋča owíčhiyakapi kta.
- *The numbers are arranged in a random order.*

397. wótkȟokila — *driven* — Used to describe something or someone that is driven, motivated, or determined.
- Hánhepi kiŋ le wótkȟokila tȟáŋkačhagla.
- *He is very driven to succeed.*

398. wóhoye — *screeching* — Used to describe a sound that is loud, piercing, and high-pitched, resembling a screech or a scream.
- Wóhoye háŋpi kiŋ nážiŋyaŋpi.
- *The screeching wind is very eerie.*

399. zíz — *blonde* — The word 'zíz' is used to describe someone with blonde hair.
- Thípi kiŋ zíz wauŋ héčha kiŋ čhaŋhákab wauŋ
- *The house has a blonde dog and a black cat*

400. owáŋspe — *active* — Used to describe something or someone as active or in motion.
- Slolya owáŋspe kiŋ hemaca gluhaŋpi.
- *The deer is very active in the morning.*

401. oíyayA — *serial* — Used to describe something that occurs, exists, or is arranged in a series or sequence.
- Iyápi kiŋ el oíyayA nape.
- *These numbers are serial.*

402. yáyaŋka — *wailing* — Used to describe a person or animal wailing loudly or mournfully.
- Makhik'iyé wíŋyan yáyaŋka kštó.
- *The grieving woman is wailing loudly.*

403. oíwakȟe — *helpful* — The word 'oíwakȟe' means 'helpful' and is used to describe people, actions, or things that are beneficial or supportive in nature.
- Tokel ya umá
- *My friend is very helpful.*

404. okál'Owa — *safely* — Used to describe something done in a safe manner or a state of being safe.
- Ní okál'Owa' kta kin hwoheya.
- *I will drive safely.*

405. iyohlogde — *upper* — The Lakota Adjective 'iyohlogde' is used to describe objects or locations that are situated at a higher or upper position.
- Hé aŋpétu iyohlogde čhaŋté ama wólowahe.
- *The sun rises in the upper part of the sky.*

406. šiča — *burnt* — Used to describe something that has been burned, charred, or scorched.
- Šiča čhokáta pi, tȟawáwa kiŋ.
- *The burnt wood is not usable.*

407. iyókȟaŋ — *happily* — Used to describe someone feeling happiness or pleasure in a situation.

- Niwíčhayapi 'iyókȟaŋ'.
- *I am living happily.*

---

408. asní — *shaking* — Used to describe something that is shaking or in a state of trembling.
- Wíčhayis éyakapta asní.
- *The tree is shaking.*

---

409. olówan — *musical* — Used to describe something that is musical or related to music.
- Wíyaye thešóya olówan.
- *He enjoys listening to musical instruments.*

---

410. ȟtayetu — *magnificent* — Used to describe something or someone as magnificent, impressive, or awe-inspiring.
- Heȟáka ȟtayetu kiŋ.
- *The mountain is magnificent.*

---

411. čȟítȟola — *enormous* — Used to describe something as being extremely large or enormous in size.
- Tȟéča wakȟáŋ čȟítȟola kiŋ hí.
- *The sacred mountain is enormous.*

---

412. téča — *raw* — The word 'téča' is used to describe something that is raw or uncooked. It can refer to food that has not been prepared or processed.
- Wíyawapi téča kiŋ kte máza!
- *I want to eat raw meat!*

---

413. óyuspa — *fond* — Used to describe a feeling of affection or liking towards someone or something.
- Wíyaye kiŋ hí, nížiŋ óyuspa ló, kiŋ oíkičiye kiŋ hí.
- *When I see you, I feel fond towards you.*

---

414. íyušpus — *appropriate* — Used to describe something that is suitable or fitting for a particular purpose or situation.
● Lila wicóni wašté íyušpus kiŋ čha
- *The blue dress is appropriate for the party.*

---

415. ómakȟaŋ — *constantly* — Used to describe something that is happening continuously or without interruption.
● Wičháša owíčhablaha el ómakȟaŋ etuŋwaŋ hé.
- *The boy is constantly running around.*

---

416. iyóyo — *differently* — Used to describe something that is done or perceived in a way that is not the same as before or in comparison to something else.
● Wí niyé iyóyo kiŋ oká kte ló.
- *She cooks the food differently now.*

---

417. máni — *global* — Used to describe something as being global or worldwide in scope.
● Tȟuŋkášila háŋ mitȟáwa kiŋ máni kte lo.
- *The Great Spirit sees all things globally.*

---

418. kȟáŋ — *catching* — Used to describe something that is catching or capable of catching. It is typically used in the context of catching something physically or metaphorically.
● Wičháša kȟáŋ hí.
- *The man is catching it.*

---

419. iȟápta — *drawn* — Used to describe something that has been drawn or sketched.
● Héčhel kiŋ iȟápta čha.
- *She drew a picture.*

---

420. ištáwaye — *shortly* — The word 'ištáwaye' is used to indicate a short amount of time or a brief duration. It can be used to describe events that will happen soon or in the near future.

- Wíyaye ištáwaye kiŋ lená makȟáwičhayapi kin.
- *I will see you shortly at the meeting place.*

421. akinl — *halfway* — Used to describe something that is halfway or partially completed.

- Wiwanyang wakan kin iyececa yelo. Hecel' aka-cin aguyapi.
- *The sacred ceremony will begin soon. Let's meet halfway.*

422. hiŋ — *hip* — Used to describe something related to the hip, such as a hip bone or hip joint.

- Hihanniŋča kiŋ lá ȟtáŋka kiŋ hótȟayetuŋ.
- *My hip bone hurts when I walk.*

423. akís — *contrary* — Used to describe something that is opposite or contrary to what is expected or desired.

- Wíyakel kičhí akís kte. Hékta owókihal ki Dakhóta he.
- *He always does the opposite. He is contrary to the Dakota people.*

424. íyokipazo — *torn* — Used to describe something that has been ripped or torn apart.

- Wíyukšákpe yelo. Íyokipazo lé ni šni.
- *My shirt is torn. It is no longer new.*

425. iye — *abroad* — Used to describe something or someone located outside a specific area or country.

- Wašíču kiŋ 'iye' yelo.
- *The white man is abroad.*

426. óniyaŋ — *chemical* — Used to describe anything related to chemicals or chemistry.

- Wíyake ye śni héčhel úŋkelóniyaŋ.
- *She is studying chemical engineering.*

427. óma — *catholic* — The Lakota adjective 'óma' means '-catholic' in English. It describes something or someone that is related to the Catholic Church or its teachings.
● Thiyošpaye omani wasté kiŋ, caŋčhapi kte lo.
- *The Catholic family is going to church today.*

428. mni — *marine* — Used to describe something as marine or related to the sea.
● Tukté mni ecíyapi kiŋ hená.
- *They are studying marine biology.*

429. ozá — *soviet* — Used to describe something that is soviet in nature, pertaining to a system of government or organization that follows the principles of soviet socialism.
● Zaptáke ozá kte lo.
- *The council is soviet in its decisions.*

430. wóhanble — *magical* — Used to describe something that is considered magical or possessing supernatural qualities.
● Wíyaktaŋka kiŋ Wowičhákhiŋpi kte. Hecišnyečayapi kte he'é wóhanble kiŋ.
- *They performed a magical ritual. It was a truly wóhanble experience.*

431. akíŋyaŋ — *temporary* — The word 'akíŋyaŋ' is used to describe something that is only temporary, not permanent or lasting.
● Wašíču kiŋ lé ožáyapi akíŋyaŋ.
- *The snow will only stay temporarily.*

432. iŋyaŋ — *inner* — The word 'iŋyaŋ' is used to describe something that is located or existing inside of a particular thing or person.
● Wíyōkiŋyaŋpi kte kštó!
- *She has a kind heart inside!*

433. icúšte — *finest* — Used to describe something as the finest or highest quality.
- Tháŋka ógle 'icúšte' kiŋ hokšíla.
- *This is the finest horse in the herd.*

434. iyútȟapi — *softly* — Used to describe the manner in which something is done softly or gently.
- Tokáhila iyútȟapi éyuha kiŋ ló.
- *She speaks softly to the child.*

435. owáŋkaŋ — *multiple* — Used to describe multiple things or objects.
- Wí suyá ȟ'e, owáŋkaŋ lówan kičhíŋ.
- *I have three dogs, they are multiple colors.*

436. háŋtaŋhaŋ — *currently* — Used to describe something that is happening at the present moment or currently.
- Wówičakta háŋtaŋhaŋ kiŋ ló.
- *I am currently eating.*

437. osnókiye — *rising* — Used to describe something that is rising or ascending.
- Chapél kiŋ la osnókiye iyéya.
- *The sun is rising in the east.*

438. mahóta — *vast* — Used to describe something as vast or extensive, often referring to large landscapes or expansive areas.
- Čhaŋté mahóta wašté ló.
- *The land is vast and beautiful.*

439. ečháŋ — *polite* — Used to describe someone who is courteous, respectful, and well-mannered in their interactions with

others.
- Wíyakȟa ečháŋ kiŋ hokáȟpta eyá.
- *He is always polite and respectful to everyone.*

---

440. íye — *constant* — Used to describe something as constant or unchanging.
- Wicíyepi kiŋ dakȟotipi.
- *The sun is constant.*

---

441. akíŋ — *backwards* — Used to describe something that is in the opposite direction or facing the opposite way.
- Wičháša kiŋ ilákin okíuŋpi akíŋ čha.
- *The man looked backwards while walking.*

---

442. Igáŋ — *shining* — Used to describe something that is shining or giving off light. It can be used to describe both natural and man-made sources of light.
- Wí wašté Igáŋ heyápi kiŋ lená akíčhetuŋ čha hí.
- *The sun is shining brightly in the sky on this beautiful day.*

---

443. wazíyaŋ — *northern* — Used to describe something that is located or related to the north. It can be used to indicate direction or position.
- Háŋpa wazíyaŋ tȟáŋka kiŋ
- *The northern sky is beautiful*

---

444. sní — *unfair* — Used to describe situations or actions that are unfair, unjust, or not right.
- Wičháȟpi kiŋ sní kiŋ hé wičháȟpi kiŋ tȟašíčupi.
- *That decision was unfair to him.*

---

445. éya — *independent* — Used to describe something or someone that is independent or self-reliant.

• Háŋska wéblaska éya kiŋ
- *The child is becoming independent.*

---

446. aŋpétu — *alike* — Used to describe two or more things that are similar or alike in some way.
• Tȟašíla aŋpétu na tȟokata kiŋ.
- *These two horses look alike.*

---

447. héčhu — *traditional* — Used to describe something that is traditional or in accordance with the ways of the ancestors.
• Héčhu wakíŋyaŋ yuhá wičhóičeya.
- *She is making traditional fry bread.*

---

448. iyómakȟiŋyaŋ — *unconscious* — The word 'iyómakȟiŋyaŋ' is used to describe someone who is in a state of unconsciousness or lacking awareness.
• Wíčhuŋ kiŋ hečhel iyómakȟiŋyaŋ.
- *He is lying there unconscious.*

---

449. íwaŋyaŋ — *questioning* — Used to describe something or someone that is in a state of questioning or uncertainty.
• Tȟašíla waŋtéktena íwaŋyaŋ na mázaska kte.
- *He is questioning whether to buy the horse.*

---

450. waŋyáŋ — *immediate* — Used to describe something that is happening or existing right now, with no delay or interval.
• Waŋyáŋ kiŋ čha t'éčhila.
- *She needs help immediately.*

---

451. phézi — *broad* — Used to describe something that has a wide or broad scope or size.
• Toká phézi kiŋ ȟakála yé.
- *The river is broad and deep.*

---

452. ayútaŋ — *comic* — Used to describe something that is funny or humorous in nature.
- Wíyakel owáyuktayaŋ wóuŋglawakȟuŋpi kta ečéiya yaútaŋ.
- *The children enjoyed reading the comic book.*

453. oyáwote — *relative* — Used to describe someone or something as being related or connected in some way.
- Wíyakapta kiŋ, oyáwote šni yelo.
- *We went to town with my relative.*

454. owáŋgaye — *corporal* — The word 'owáŋgaye' is used to describe something related to the body or physical form.
- Wí blužápi kin héčha owáŋgaye yelo.
- *He has excellent corporal strength.*

455. akím — *closely* — The word 'akím' is used to describe something that is in close proximity or closely related to something else.
- Wíyak'é, éya okóičakšuŋpi wasté, akím tuktétuwašteya
- *Friend, when you have something good, it is better to keep it close.*

456. iwéčȟuŋ — *solo* — Used to describe something or someone that is alone or solitary. It conveys the idea of being by oneself or without others.
- Wíyakal ičéwičhašta iyometáwičhiŋca, íyotwaŋkiŋ, na iwéčȟuŋ hiŋháŋ.
- *She walked to her house alone, without assistance, and she arrived there solo.*

457. hoȟúŋ — *faithful* — Used to describe someone or something that is loyal, trustworthy, and reliable.
- Wóuŋspe kiŋ 'hoȟúŋ' yuha pi.
- *My dog is faithful to me.*

458. íyaŋ — *elsewhere* — The word 'íyaŋ' is used to indicate a location that is somewhere other than the current place or a location being talked about.

● Makȟášiča kiŋ ún éyapaha čhaŋ lá 'íyaŋ' tȟáŋka.
- *I left my phone somewhere else.*

459. ómani — *martial* — The word 'ómani' is used to describe something related to fighting or war, often referring to martial arts or combat skills.

● WíyayA yeya ómani kta he
- *He is training in martial arts.*

460. okíle — *humble* — Used to describe someone who has a modest and unassuming demeanor.

● Waníyetu wašté okíle yelo.
- *He is a good and humble person.*

461. ohánke — *overnight* — Used to describe something that happens or lasts for the duration of the night.

● Wíkoskaye ohánke kiŋ taŋyáŋka oíyokiyaŋpi.
- *I will stay overnight in the mountains.*

462. híŋtaŋ — *fairly* — Used to indicate something is done to a moderate or reasonable extent.

● Wíčhakiyapi híŋtaŋ ijáyuŋhaŋ yahi.
- *He speaks Lakota fairly well.*

463. čhéyaŋ — *adorable* — In Lakota, the adjective 'čhéyaŋ' is used to describe something or someone as adorable or cute. It conveys a sense of endearment and charm.

● Héčhe čhéyaŋ kiŋ hokšíla.
- *My little puppy is adorable.*

464. níyuŋ — *specifically* — Used to emphasize that something is being referred to in a specific or particular manner.
- Háŋ níyuŋ wíyelo kiŋ haŋpí.
- *I specifically want the blue one.*

---

465. tótȟapi — *luckily* — Used to describe a fortunate or lucky situation.
- Tótȟapi, kiŋ čha wówahwakto!
- *Luckily, we found the lost keys!*

---

466. iyéčhala — *anonymous* — The Lakota adjective 'iyéčhala' means 'anonymous' or 'unidentified'. It is used to describe someone or something that is not known or recognized by name or identity.
- Wašté iyéčhala kiŋ kahníyetu.
- *He received an anonymous gift.*

---

467. iyóyaŋ — *operating* — Used to describe something that is currently in operation or functioning.
- Wíčhuŋkičiyapi kiŋ itókiyaŋ hé iyóyaŋ.
- *The computer is currently operating and functioning well.*

---

468. ištíma — *visual* — Used to describe something related to sight or vision. It indicates that the noun it is describing is something that can be seen or perceived visually.
- Héčhel ištíma kiŋ čhaŋ'ákiyapi kiŋ ló.
- *The painting is very visual.*

---

469. yawá — *content* — Used to describe the feeling of being satisfied or at peace with a situation or circumstance.
- Wíyaye yawá kiŋ láktuŋwaŋ yuȟaŋ yamníyaŋpi.
- *I am content with how the ceremony turned out.*

---

470. iyáŋ — *remaining* — Used to describe something that is left or remaining after others have been removed or used up.
- Wíčháklu iyáŋ hé kiŋ thókšič'iyéča.
- *There is only a little food remaining in the pot.*

---

471. čhetúŋ — *oldest* — Used to describe the oldest member of a group or the oldest in age.
- Wí tuwaša čhetúŋ kiŋ hí.
- *She is the oldest sister.*

---

472. šíčamna — *mere* — Used to describe something as being mere or simply that thing, emphasizing that it is not significant or of much importance.
- Wakȟáŋ šní ǧíkčipiju ayašíčamna.
- *The sacred pipe is used for mere talking.*

---

473. takú — *primary* — Used to describe something that is primary or the first in a series or order.
- Tokáhe takú kiŋ čhaŋ, tókȟa kiŋ ȟáŋkayeyapi.
- *The primary reason for this is that he is too young.*

---

474. wíyopiyǎ — *shitty* — Used to describe something of poor quality or undesirable. It can be used to express displeasure or disappointment.
- Igmu ka wíyopiyǎ.
- *This food is shitty.*

---

475. Igáŋtaŋ — *roaring* — Used to describe something that is making a loud, deep, and continuous sound, similar to the roar of a lion or the sound of a strong wind.
- Wíčhaša ecíyapi Igáŋtaŋ yuha kiŋ le.
- *The bear is roaring loudly in the forest.*

476. owápahmi — *alternative* — Used to describe something that serves as an alternative or substitute.
• Iyápi kte lo owápahmi kičhíŋ čha.
- *I will use the alternative route instead.*

477. iyéya — *attacking* — Used to describe something that is attacking or aggressive in nature.
• Wílowaháŋ iyéya kiŋ
- *The warrior is attacking the enemy*

478. owášteča — *surprising* — Used to describe something that is unexpected or surprising.
• Hečáku owášteča kiŋ čhaŋlá wópila.
- *The sudden storm was surprising and beautiful.*

479. t'ó — *tender* — Used to describe something that is soft, gentle, or delicate in texture. It conveys a sense of tenderness and delicacy.
• Wówaži t'ó kiŋ, kiŋlúla šni.
- *The baby's skin is tender and soft.*

480. owákahni — *significant* — Used to describe something as significant or meaningful.
• Wíle úŋiháŋ mnišní owákahni yelo.
- *This ceremony is very significant.*

481. wówaŋyaŋg — *corporate* — Used to describe something as being corporate or related to a corporation or business entity.
• Tȟaŋí pi kte lúta iyá wówaŋyaŋg kagláska kta henáhpapi.
- *They are going to start a corporate training program soon.*

482. mat'éče — *keen* — Used to describe someone who is attentive, sharp, or perceptive in their observations or actions.

- Wí waštélkiyA aní čha 'mat'éče' waštél.
- *I am very keen to learn how to speak Lakota.*

---

483. t'óka — *vain* — Used to describe something or someone that is vain or full of pride.
- Waníyetu kiŋ lé t'óka.
- *He is very vain.*

---

484. wolákíč'uŋ — *neat* — Used to describe something that is tidy, organized, or well put together.
- Wolákíč'uŋ čhaŋtétuŋpi kte sní.
- *You have a neat and clean room.*

---

485. iyéčetu — *accidentally* — Used to describe an action or event that happens by chance or without intention, often referred to as 'accidentally'.
- Wí kiŋ ógle iyéčetu kiŋ keyákiya héčhetu.
- *I spilled water accidentally on the floor.*

---

486. oyáte wówaši — *pacific* — Used to describe something or someone as peaceful or pacific in the Lakota language.
- Osíčeya kiŋ lenápi wóuŋope oyáte wówaši.
- *The community gathered together for a peaceful protest.*

---

487. čhaŋkíč'uŋ — *kindly* — The word 'čhaŋkíč'uŋ' is used to describe actions or behaviors that are done in a kind and considerate manner towards others.
- Wopíla čhaŋkíč'uŋ kiŋ kštó.
- *Thank you for speaking kindly.*

---

488. kíčiwíčhakča — *electronic* — The word 'kíčiwíčhakča' is used to describe anything related to electronics or technology.
- Mní kïpoda kíčiwíčhakča lúta uŋkíŋ yamní wáyetu.
- *I bought a new electronic phone yesterday.*

489. t'óče — *bare* — Used to describe something that is bare or naked, lacking covering or clothing.
- Wí, he éčhe s'át'óče.
- *Yes, the tree is bare.*

490. owájikale — *blank* — Used to describe something as blank or empty, lacking content or information.
- Héhaší šni oyájikale.
- *The paper is blank.*

491. owíčazi — *glorious* — Used to describe something as magnificent or prestigious, often implying a sense of beauty and grandeur.
- Wakíŋya šni hé owíčazi čha.
- *The sky is truly glorious today.*

492. wówaši — *practicing* — The Lakota adjective 'wówaši' means 'practicing', typically used to describe someone who is actively engaged in learning or training something.
- Nahátuŋšila wówaši cha tȟál wówaši hečíya.
- *He is practicing writing and speaking.*

493. čhaŋtéšila — *genuine* — The Lakota adjective 'čhaŋtéšila' means 'genuine' and is used to describe something that is truly authentic or real.
- Aŋpétu waštéya čhaŋtéšila omniciyépi kiŋ hečíya.
- *The sunrise is a genuine reminder of a new day.*

494. ohíye — *bold* — The Lakota adjective 'ohíye' means 'bold' and is used to describe someone who is brave, daring, or fearless in their actions or beliefs.
- Wí yeló. Ohíyelo tka.
- *Do not be afraid. Be bold.*

495. waŋuŋka — *risky* — Used to describe something that is risky or dangerous.
● Waŋuŋka kiŋ lená wópeya.
- *It is risky to walk on the ice.*

496. otéwaye — *formal* — Used to describe something that is done in a formal manner or conforms to traditional customs and protocols.
● Nahéglížapi kiŋ wíyaye kin bí. Wowáškiča hékta yamní 'otéwaye' došniyé kiŋ.
- *She always speaks in a formal manner. The ceremony was very 'otéwaye'.*

497. čhantó — *somewhat* — Used to express a degree of something, meaning 'somewhat' or 'a little'. It is used to indicate that something is not fully or completely the described quality, but is somewhat close to it.
● Wakíŋya čhantó ečéča kičhíčiyayapi.
- *The horse is somewhat fast.*

498. šíč'uŋ — *slight* — Used to describe something that is slight or small in degree or amount.
● Čhaŋšbe yelo wana šíč'uŋ ye.
- *The sun is shining slightly.*

499. wanaží — *handy* — Used to describe something that is convenient or useful for a specific purpose.
● Niáčapi wanaží kta.
- *I need a handy tool.*

500. tuwéča — *anyways* — Used to transition to a different topic or to indicate that the speaker is moving on with the conversation.

- Wíčhuȟupi kiŋ tuwéča yámni čha tȟáŋkala.
- *I don't like that movie anyways.*

---

501. wókaǧe — *outer* — Used to describe something that is on the outside or exterior of something else.
- Waȟpéya wókaǧe kiŋ hé uŋčhíŋpi kte.
- *The red outer part of the apple is sour.*

---

502. kíčíȷ̌ašká — *electrical* — Used to describe things that are related to electricity or have an electrical charge.
- Wašté kíčíȷ̌ašká čík'ala yelo!
- *The electrical light is very bright!*

---

503. wówače — *technical* — Used to describe something that is related to technology or requires technical knowledge and skills.
- Wówače kiŋ lená wóčhe kiŋ he kštó.
- *This technical problem is difficult to solve.*

---

504. wazí — *imperial* — Used to describe something that is associated with or resembles an empire.
- Héčha wazí kiŋ lenápaha yo!
- *This city looks imperial!*

---

505. wókičhuŋyaŋ — *convenient* — Used to describe something that is easy to use or helpful in making tasks easier.
- Iyáȟčičaga wókičhuŋyaŋ nážipe.
- *This tool is very convenient.*

---

506. iyétokčaŋ — *maximum* — Used to describe the highest level or amount of something.
- Šnób okówaŋna iyétokčaŋ glinípi kte lo.
- *He reached the maximum level in his performance.*

---

507. wakíč'uŋ — *secretly* — Used to describe something that is done in a secretive or hidden manner.
- Wakíč'uŋ hečhá maká kiŋ lená wóphila.
- *He gave her a gift secretly.*

508. wóokčaŋ — *almighty* — Used to describe something or someone as being all-powerful or having ultimate authority and control.
- Wóokčaŋ hečíyela yelo.
- *He is considered to be almighty.*

509. čháŋ — *woody* — Used to describe something that is woody or made of wood. It can be used to refer to trees, wooden objects, or anything else that has a woody texture or appearance.
- The čháŋ čhúŋkú is tall and strong.
- *The woody tree is tall and strong.*

510. čhaŋzi — *sleepy* — Used to describe the feeling of being sleepy or drowsy.
- Wóuŋspe čhaŋzi kiŋ hčhetuŋpi.
- *The child is feeling sleepy now.*

511. čhaŋtéwaste — *dearest* — Used to express endearment towards someone or something, translating to 'dearest' in English.
- Wíyakȟa čhaŋtéwaste kiŋ lila.
- *She is my dearest friend.*

512. owášič'a — *instrumental* — Used to describe something that is instrumental, or a tool used to accomplish a task or goal.
- Wíyawapi kiŋ yná owášič'a táku yeló.
- *I will use this instrument to fix it.*

513. šíč'utȟaŋka — *rarely* — The word 'šíč'utȟaŋka' is used to describe something that happens or exists very infrequently or rarely.

• 'Wíčhaša waniyetu wíyakel un ké pí yel ómnipi, šíč'utȟaŋka o-kiyúza.'

- *During the winter, I rarely see a bear because they hibernate.*

---

514. owíyokiphi — *economic* — The word 'owíyokiphi' is used to describe things related to finances, money, or economy.

• Owíyokiphi kiŋ le gle pačiyé lo, níčiŋe wíyuhpe kiŋ okó wé a-kicita šni.

- *The economic situation in our country is not stable.*

---

515. owíčhak'a — *loudly* — Used to describe something that is done with a high volume or intensity, typically pertaining to sound or speech.

• Wíčhaša owíčhak'a kiŋ lenážiŋ kte.

- *The man is speaking loudly.*

---

516. ičháŋska — *originally* — The word 'ičháŋska' is used to describe something that is original or existed in its first form.

• Wašté wačhíčhila kičhíčiyaya ožúlopi waštépe. Ičháŋska kin š-ni

- *The beautiful dress was originally made with blue beads. It is original.*

---

517. kíčiwičháŋ — *sworn* — Used to describe something that has been promised or pledged in a formal or solemn manner.

• Héčhetu kíčiwičháŋ owáye kiŋ lená tótalazapì.

- *He always keeps his sworn word.*

---

518. tȟaŋíč'uŋ — *domestic* — Used to describe something that is related to the home or household, such as domestic animals or domestic chores.

- Wíyuȟapi kičhíta tȟaŋíč'uŋ wašíču kte lo.
- *I cooked domestic beef for dinner.*

519. wolášte — *tasty* — The word 'wolášte' is used to describe food or drinks that are pleasing to the taste buds, typically referring to something that is delicious or flavorful.
- Heȟíǧa welóšte kiŋ okihiča.
- *This soup is very tasty.*

520. woíyokiphi — *legally* — Used to describe something that is done according to the law or within the limits of the law.
- Olowan ma'za woíyokiphi k'ékiyemniya.
- *He handled the situation legally.*

521. wolášteča — *jolly* — Used to describe someone who is merry, cheerful, or jolly.
- Wolášteča kiŋ čhaŋté waúŋ.
- *She is always jolly.*

522. owíčhakič'a — *proven* — Used to describe something that has been demonstrated or confirmed to be true or accurate.
- Háŋ owíčhakič'a kiŋ hečhel uŋyétuŋyaŋ yelo.
- *The experiment has been proven to be successful.*

523. woǧíŋza — *inviting* — The word 'woǧíŋza' means 'inviting' in English. It is used to describe a welcoming or hospitable atmosphere or a person who is warm and friendly.
- Haŋska woǧíŋza Hečíya pi haŋska čhaŋtétuyaŋkel.
- *The house is inviting and we are happy to be here.*

524. taŋhúškila — *essential* — Used to describe something that is necessary or vital.
- Wóiyowasté kiŋ he éluȟa waŋ taŋhúškila.
- *Water is essential for life.*

525. kičúŋti — *nearest* — Used to describe the nearest object or person in relation to something else.
● Hé kičúŋti he k'úŋ yaȟpá kte.
- *He bought the nearest house.*

526. kaŋ — *horny* — Used to describe a feeling of being sexually aroused or wanting sexual activity.
● WíčhíyAkaŋ na.
- *I am feeling horny.*

527. taŋišila — *ultimately* — The adjective taŋišila is used to convey the idea of 'ultimately' or 'finally' in a sentence, emphasizing the ultimate result or outcome of a particular action or event.
● Wíyayapi taŋišila kiŋ uŋglíiŋ yeló.
- *I finally found my keys.*

528. wówaksa — *elegant* — Used to describe something as - elegant, graceful, or stylish.
● Wówaksa čhokátapi kte le eháŋni.
- *She dances with elegant movements.*

529. owíkič'aŋka — *blaring* — Used to describe a loud, piercing sound or noise that is obtrusive and attention-grabbing.
● Wíčhákhi kiŋ hí uŋglúkta owíkič'aŋka kiŋ he?
- *Why is that alarm blaring so loudly?*

530. yamníkaŋ — *triple* — Used to describe something that is three times the usual amount or size. It conveys the idea of triple or threefold.
● Wí Thípi kiŋ óglúška yamníkaŋ kte lo.
- *There are three dogs in the house.*

531. oltéwaye — *logical* — Used to describe something that is logical or reasonable in a systematic and orderly manner.
● Hečílečupi kiŋ le oltéwaye kiŋ lenáhel.
- *She always approaches problems in a logical way.*

532. waŋíčaŋ — *mutual* — Used to describe a relationship, agreement, or action that involves mutual participation or benefit from both parties.
● Waŋíčaŋ kiŋ hečápi kte.
- *They worked together.*

533. zičá — *blond* — Used to describe something or someone as blond in color. It is used to specify the hair color or overall appearance of a person.
● Wíyakaske zičá kiŋ 'ayaí' un égíyaka.
- *The girl with blond hair is very beautiful.*

534. wakíčaŋ — *honorable* — Used to describe someone or something as having a reputation of being honorable, respected, or esteemed.
● Wíyaka wakíčaŋ kiŋ lákȟotaŋ wašté kiŋláŋpi.
- *He is an honorable man in the Lakota community.*

535. wówaksiča — *convincing* — Used to describe something that is convincing or persuasive in nature.
● Lakȟól'iyapi kiŋ ómakȟa wówaksiča yeló.
- *Her argument was very convincing.*

536. wakíčhakič'a — *immortal* — The Lakota adjective 'wakíčhakič'a' means 'immortal', describing something or someone that is not subject to death.
● Thiye héčhel wakíčhakič'a kiŋ ló, he is an immortal being.
- *He is an immortal being.*

537. mní — *fluid* — Used to describe something that is fluid or flowing, like water or a liquid substance.

● Mní wóglakapi kiŋ lá
- *The water is very fluid*

---

538. wíyuskinyaŋ — *biological* — The Lakota term 'wíyuskinyaŋ' is used to describe something related to biology or living organisms.

● Íyéča šni ská yo kte, wíyuskinyaŋ kiŋ na Iyásla na wípazkiyapi.
- *The study of how the body works is an important part of biology.*

---

539. kiŋháŋl — *consistent* — The word 'kiŋháŋl' is used to describe something that is consistent or remains the same over time.

● Wičháša kiŋháŋl čhaŋte hé iyéča.
- *The man consistently takes care of his horse.*

---

540. lechel — *awhile* — Used to indicate a period of time that is extended or longer than just a moment.

● Olowan lechel eyamayan kte lo.
- *He sang for awhile.*

---

541. ozí — *shiny* — Used to describe something that is shiny or reflective, suggesting a polished or gleaming appearance.

● Wí yuhápi ozí kiŋ híštaya.
- *The car looks shiny in the sunlight.*

---

542. owáyakapi — *cultural* — Used to describe something related to a particular culture or cultural practices.

● Hčhémni kičhitsu owáyakapi thí
- *They practice their cultural traditions*

---

543. wóeyawiya — *terrifying* — The term 'wóeyawiya' is used to describe something that causes fear or dread in a person. It signifies a sense of terror or horror.

- Wańi ǧíǧa wóeyawiya kte.
- *The dark forest is terrifying.*

544. wanáyiŋ — *conscious* — Used to describe something or someone as being conscious, aware, or mindful.
- Wičhówaŋ wanáyiŋ héčhe tuwayeža kiŋ hékta wóihaŋke.
- *The horse is conscious of the fact that he needs to follow the leader.*

545. ostéča — *identical* — Used to describe two or more things that are identical or indistinguishable from each other.
- Wíyayekiya owókiya ostéča ya kéča kiŋ hé kiŋ.
- *The twin sisters look identical to each other.*

546. thokáhe ókihi — *mainly* — The phrase 'thokáhe ókihi' is used to indicate something that is primarily or predominantly the case.
- Wíphope thokáhe ókihi wašté kiŋ héktaŋ.
- *He mainly eats healthy food.*

547. owíčhathuŋ — *industrial* — Used to describe something related to industry or industrial activities.
- Wíyukšápaye owíčhathuŋ kiŋ le iháŋska ogná weló.
- *The factory is located in the industrial area.*

548. oíhimna — *confidential* — Used to describe something - that is kept secret or private, not to be shared with others.
- Wakíŋya yuá oíhimna kičhíčaku le thaŋka na wí po.
- *The eagle told me something confidential.*

549. iyóku — *mentally* — Used to describe something related to the mind or mental processes.
- Wakíkiye iyóku kiŋ lá waŋglakápi kta kiŋ he?
- *Why are you mentally tired today?*

550. okáhni oíhanke — *importantly* — The word 'okáhni oíhanke' is used to emphasize the importance of something.
• Wíyuhapi tóna úŋkiksuyéya okáhni oíhanke.
- *It is important to always be kind.*

551. khéčhiyela — *rattling* — Used to describe something that is making a rattling sound.
• Wíčhaša khéčhiyela kiŋ lá uŋsní čha okíyakapo.
- *The man heard the rattling noise in the bushes.*

552. owákahŋ — *sentimental* — The term 'owákahŋ' is used to describe feelings of deep affection or nostalgia towards a person, place, or thing.
• Wíŋyaŋpi kičhí owákahŋ yeló.
- *I feel sentimental about my hometown.*

553. čhaŋkál — *youngest* — The word 'čhaŋkál' is used to describe the youngest person or thing in a group or family.
• Wašté čhaŋkál elí! Háŋ, ecíyapi.
- *Look at the youngest! Wow, how they've grown.*

554. tȟaŋháŋ — *organic* — Used to describe something that is organic, natural, or derived from living organisms.
• Wíčhayapi čháŋtȟatȟáŋ tȟaŋháŋ wóžupi kiŋ lé.
- *I prefer to eat organic vegetables.*

555. wíčhaleča — *occasionally* — Used to describe something that happens from time to time, not regularly or consistently.
• Ihanblaska šni khéya yuún 'wíčhaleča' hí.
- *I see him at the store 'occasionally'.*

556. íčhiyutȟaŋ — *promising* — íčhiyutȟaŋ' is used to describe something or someone that shows great potential for success

or achievement in the future.
- Tokákiye héčhel wóihaŋblonakhiŋ he iyéčhiyutȟaŋ.
- *The young artist has a promising future.*

---

557. wíwičhakičhiyaka — *amusing* — The Lakota adjective - 'wíwičhakičhiyaka' describes something that is entertaining or delightful in a humorous way.
- Wíwičhakičhiyaka ispi kte lo.
- *He is very amusing.*

---

558. wítokšila — *relevant* — Used to describe something that is pertinent or applicable to a particular situation or topic.
- Kíčhe hdákotayé wítokšila kiŋ ló.
- *This information is relevant to the Dakota People.*

---

559. waháŋna — *representative* — The word 'waháŋna' is used to describe something or someone that serves as a representative or symbol of a larger group or idea.
- He is considered the waháŋna of our tribe.
- *Hé iyél wíyanke waháŋna hečéla.*

---

560. ihékta — *objective* — Used to describe something that is objective or unbiased, free from personal opinions or feelings.
- Waŋží iyá ihékta čhiyúziŋsni.
- *He presents a very objective argument.*

---

561. wakíhu — *modest* — The word 'wakíhu' is used to describe someone who is humble and modest in their actions and demeanor.
- Wíčhíyela wakíhu uŋyápi kiŋ čha tȟáŋka.
- *She always dresses modestly.*

---

562. owíthukča — *deliberately* — Used to describe actions or decisions that are done intentionally or with purpose.

● Wíčhuȟa owíthukča kiŋ ní.
- *He spoke deliberately.*

---

563. waštéča — *automatic* — The Lakota adjective 'waštéča' means 'automatic' and is used to describe something that functions or operates by itself or with little to no external control.
● Iyápi waštéča kiŋ heíč'ayetu keyápi.
- *The door opens automatically.*

---

564. šiyohe — *legitimate* — Used to describe something that is legitimate or valid according to cultural or societal norms.
● Wakinyan wašte sni hečhahu, ka šiyohe kiŋ.
- *The eagle feather is good, it is legitimate to wear it.*

---

565. wičháyapi — *alcoholic* — Used to describe someone who is an alcoholic, or someone who consumes alcohol excessively.
● Híčhiyaka wičháyapi yelo.
- *He is an alcoholic.*

---

566. opȟéyatka — *compound* — Used to describe something that is compound or complex, made up of multiple elements or parts.
● Wíyayaye kéto opȟéyatka kiŋ oíchel wowapi na tȟawílakapí - kte lo.
- *I read a compound book that had both pictures and text.*

---

567. oínažiŋ — *supporting* — Used to describe something or someone that is providing support or assistance.
● Wíyaka oínažiŋ yé.
- *He is supporting the tree.*

---

568. owáekiyapi — *beautifully* — The word 'owáekiyapi' is u-sed to describe something as beautiful or pleasing to the eye.
● Wíčhayetupi owáekiyapi kiŋ lé, ómakȟa takúŋkiyapi kin hena

sni.
- *The sunset is beautifully colorful, painting the sky in shades of red.*

---

569. hokšíče — *freely* — The word 'hokšíče' is used to describe an action or state of being done freely, without constraint or hesitation.
- Wóuŋspe kiŋ lé hokšíče yéčeya.
- *He walks freely in the forest.*

---

570. iyóšiča — *classical* — Used to describe something as classical or traditional, often referring to music, art, or literature that is considered to be of high quality and longstanding significance.
- Hečáke, wíyowiyakel iyóšiča oblayečheyapi kta.
- *Today, we will listen to classical music.*

---

571. makíkčiŋ — *pressing* — Used to describe something that is pressing or urgent, indicating that it requires immediate attention.
- Híŋhe makíkčiŋ kte ló, wóphaŋže kiŋ.
- *It's pressing, we need to hurry.*

---

572. iyókiphi — *emotionally* — Used to describe something - relating to emotions or feelings.
- Wíyuze oíyuha na iyókiphi kiŋyáŋpi kte he?
- *Why are you acting so emotionally today?*

---

573. išáŋhna — *visible* — Used to describe something that is able to be seen or perceived with the eyes.
- Tokáhe išáŋhna kiŋ lená.
- *The horse is visible on the hill.*

---

574. oíke — *outstanding* — The word 'oíke' is used to describe something or someone that is exceptional or outstanding in a

positive way.
- Hé hí oíke kiŋ, na ptehíŋčha kiŋ ló.
- *He is outstanding at singing and dancing.*

---

575. mičhá — *underwater* — Used to describe something that is located or happening underwater.
- Mní mičhá čháŋ t'óópila.
- *The fish is swimming underwater.*

---

576. wólayapi — *developing* — Used to describe something that is developing or progressing over time.
- Waúŋšila wówičhake lená akíčhiyapi wólayapi.
- *My child is growing and developing rapidly.*

---

577. iwízi — *delightful* — The word 'iwízi' is used to describe something that brings pleasure or happiness. It is often used to express a sense of enjoyment or positivity.
- Wíyake owígé 'iwízi' kte.
- *The meal was delightful.*

---

578. itȟóthi — *subtle* — The word 'itȟóthi' is used to describe something that is delicate and not easily perceived or understood.
- Waníyetu na itȟóthi ókiyakapi.
- *The winter sky is subtly beautiful.*

---

579. iwáhetena — *magnetic* — Used to describe something that is magnetic, attracting or having the ability to draw in other objects or people.
- Thípi kte hípi kin héecpiya eyá iyeča, iyúzape táku iyáyani kte šni. Thípi kta táku iwáhetena.
- *When we walk by that house, it feels like something is pulling us towards it. That house is magnetic.*

---

580. owákatuya — *elite* — Used to describe something or someone as 'elite', signifying a position of superiority or excellence.
● Wíyanpi na owákatuya kiŋ ní haŋ síča na kála.
- *She belongs to an elite family.*

581. ičhániptȟapi — *ambitious* — The Lakota adjective 'ičhániptȟapi' describes someone who has a strong desire to achieve their goals and succeed in life.
● WíyakA iyéčhiyA čhéyA kičhániptȟapiyA sní áta hwohátakiyA.
- *She is very ambitious and always works hard to achieve her goals.*

582. wahónapi — *heavenly* — Used to describe something that is heavenly or divine in nature.
● Wióhpe waú, wahónapi kiŋláya.
- *The stars in the sky are heavenly.*

583. niyúŋka — *controlling* — The Lakota adjective 'niyúŋka' describes something or someone that has the ability to control or manage a situation.
● Wí híŋhaŋniyaŋke yelo niyúŋka pi naíŋ wičhaša owíće.
- *She is a good leader because she is controlling and responsible.*

584. iyókiyapi — *respectable* — Used to describe someone or something as being respectable, honorable, or worthy of respect.
● Wíyan wóuŋslila iyókiyapi kiŋ hečhíŋ.
- *The elderly woman is very respectable and wise.*

585. lečháŋ — *casual* — Used to describe something casual or informal in nature.
● Šni aŋpétu lečháŋ hí.
- *I am wearing casual clothes.*

586. išáŋkhota — *protective* — Used to describe something that provides protection or security.
- Máza isáŋkhota kiŋ hena yuŋyáŋpi kte lo.
- *The fence is protective because it keeps strangers out.*

587. owíčha — *intent* — Used to describe someone or something with a deliberate or purposeful intention.
- Wópila ye, owíčha kiŋ hečhel o úŋkitȟuŋ.
- *Thank you, I appreciate your intent to help.*

588. wóiyukhaŋ — *surrounding* — Used to describe something that surrounds or encircles another object or person.
- Híŋhaŋni kte wóiyukhaŋ sápi yamnípi kte.
- *The fence surrounds the black horse.*

589. na! — *instantly* — The word 'na!' is used to convey immediacy or suddenness, similar to the English word 'instantly'. It adds emphasis to the quickness of an action.
- Nake wana unkispe na!
- *I will arrive instantly!*

590. phisíŋ — *hairy* — The word 'phisíŋ' is used to describe something or someone that has a lot of hair, such as an animal or a person with long or thick hair.
- Wahúŋbla ogná phisíŋ tȟáŋka kte.
- *The bear is very hairy.*

591. hoǧá — *stinking* — Used to describe something that has a foul or unpleasant smell.
- Wíkcuṭa čhúŋka hoǧá yeló.
- *The buffalo dung is stinking.*

592. owáwašte — *gracious* — The word 'owáwašte' is used to describe someone who is kind, considerate, and showing a willi-

ngness to help others. It is a term of praise for someone who is generous and caring.
- Wóphila owáwašte kiŋ lé wičhóič'iyá.
- *Thank you for being gracious to me.*

---

593. inážiŋ — *demanding* — Used to describe someone or something that is demanding, whether it be in terms of time, effort, or resources.
- Wíčhaša inážiŋ kiŋ
- *The man is demanding*

---

594. iyóyakapi — *flowing* — Used to describe something that is flowing, such as water or a river.
- Mnišničhíŋ iyóyakapi kiŋ
- *The river is flowing*

---

595. iwákin — *stunning* — Used to describe something that is visually striking or impressive, often in a positive way.
- Héčha kiŋ iháŋzitakiyapi kiŋ, išté iyákin.
- *The sunset tonight is stunning.*

---

596. iyómakhaŋ — *exotic* — Used to describe something that is of foreign or unfamiliar origin, often perceived as exotic.
- Wíyuhapi iyómakhaŋ nážiŋ kiŋ héčečhe wé om aká wóihaŋke kiŋ.
- *The woman wore exotic jewelry to the party.*

---

597. owašlí — *fitting* — Used to describe something that is appropriate or suitable for a specific situation or purpose.
- Wíye owašlí kiŋ lákȟotiyapi yužápi.
- *This book is fitting for learning Lakota.*

---

598. owáyečin — *gladly* — Used to describe a feeling of joy or happiness when doing something willingly or eagerly.

- WíčhayA owáyečin wayéčhiyA kičhímakA yúhá.
- *I will gladly help you with your work.*

---

599. owáhiyeya — *efficient* — Used to describe something that is effective or working well in achieving its intended purpose.
- Iyéčhel čha owáhiyeya kiŋ.
- *This tool is very efficient.*

---

600. owášté — *compromised* — Used to describe something that has been compromised or affected negatively in some way.
- Tokáhe owášté kiŋ, hečhá kiŋ šni.
- *The food is compromised, do not eat it.*

---

601. wanaǧi — *destined* — Used to describe something that is destined or meant to happen in the future.
- Wanaǧi kiŋ: he miče wastépi kičhiyaye.
- *Destined to come: the best is yet to come.*

---

602. wahíyaye — *legendary* — Wahíyaye is used to describe something or someone with great significance or fame within Lakota legend or tradition.
- Čhaŋté waŋyáŋpi ečhéčha wahíyaye yamní.
- *The story of the good-hearted wolf is legendary.*

---

603. ipá — *printed* — Used to describe something that has been printed or is in a printed format.
- Lápi owíyóita ipá kiŋ lená, hékta el óyaŋke héčha kiŋ kte.
- *The newspaper I am reading is printed in color, it looks very nice.*

---

604. iyókihi — *grounded* — The adjective 'iyókihi' in Lakota means 'grounded', referring to someone who is stable, balanced, and connected to the earth.
- Wokíčhuŋža iyókihi yelo.
- *The tree is grounded.*

605. oktáŋwaŋ — *lined* — Used to describe something that has lines or stripes running horizontally or vertically.
• Iyéčhiya kiŋ lóhto oktáŋwaŋ hečá sá spíyahiŋpi.
- *The shirt that I bought has a lined pattern on it.*

606. iŋzí — *incoming* — Used to describe something or someone that is coming towards a certain location.
• Tokata kiŋ la iŋzí.
- *The enemy is incoming towards the camp.*

607. owáktomni — *contained* — Used to describe something that is contained within a specific place or object.
• Wíkuwakta owáktomniŋičiye.
- *The water is contained in the bottle.*

608. okšá — *shattered* — Used to describe something that is broken into pieces or shattered.
• Akíŋ kiŋ la okšá šni.
- *The glass is shattered.*

609. oíyote — *hereby* — Used to indicate something that is being done or agreed to at the present moment or being stated in the current context. It is used to emphasize that something is being done formally or officially.
• Wíčhíyaye oíyote kiŋ henápi kiŋ adá k'éǧiŋ t'áŋgle kiŋ.
- *I hereby declare that this land belongs to us.*

610. Ýápi — *rapidly* — Used to describe something that is done quickly or at a fast pace.
• Mní wóglakel ýápi kiŋ.
- *He is drinking water rapidly.*

611. yuwíŋyaŋ — *listed* — Used to describe something that has been put on a list or formally recorded.

• Mazaska yuwíŋyaŋ.

- *The money is listed.*

---

612. owáyesica — *thoughtful* — The word 'owáyesica' describes someone who is considerate and mindful in their actions and decisions.

• Wítaŋgle owáyesica kiŋ hena taku kte lo.

- *She always acts thoughtful and does what is right.*

---

613. owáčhičhiyA — *forensic* — Used to describe something or someone related to forensic science or investigation.

• Wózupi wátašni kte ló. OwáčhičhiyA kiŋ léčiyA kta kštó.

- *They are going to investigate the case. The forensic team will arrive soon.*

---

614. wičháwalakapi — *flattered* — The word 'wičháwalakapi' is used to describe the feeling of being flattered or complimented.

• Ate waúŋšila hí le, ní wičháwalakapi čha.

- *When they praised me, I felt flattered.*

---

615. okíyakapi — *overseas* — Used to describe something or someone that is located or originating from overseas.

• Hánblečeya okíyakapi kiŋ háŋ.

- *The ship is from overseas.*

---

616. iyówašte — *universal* — Used to describe something that is universal or applicable to all individuals or situations.

• Wakíčuŋ kte lo iyówašte kiŋ

- *Love is universal for everyone*

---

617. owášteče — *supposedly* — Used to indicate that something is supposed or believed to be true, but may not necessarily

be so.
- Išta waŋblí kiŋ owášteče yeló.
- *I heard that it is supposedly going to snow.*

---

618. wichá — *mini* — Used to describe something as being - small or mini in size.
- Wichá čiíla kiŋ kštó.
- *The mini horse is fast.*

---

619. ikčháŋ — *continuing* — Used to describe something that is ongoing or continuing without interruption.
- Wíwanyake ikčháŋ eyápi kte.
- *The rain is continuing to fall.*

---

620. owáštečhila — *advised* — The Lakota adjective 'owáštečhila' means 'advised', indicating that the subject has been given advice or guidance.
- Wí mákča owáštečhila kičhízapi kte.
- *The young man listened to the advice.*

---

621. iwakhíhiyuŋ — *accepting* — The Lakota adjective 'iwakhíhiyuŋ' describes someone who is accepting of a situation or willing to receive something without resistance.
- Wíyuke iyápi kiŋ le, úŋiyapi iwakhíhiyuŋ yelo.
- *Even though it is difficult, she is accepting the truth.*

---

622. owákte — *improved* — Used to describe something that has been made better or enhanced.
- WíyayA wayáwa owákte kiŋ kte.
- *The house looks improved after the renovations.*

---

623. owóthuŋ — *baked* — Used to describe something that has been baked or cooked in an oven.

• Unyám owótȟuŋ kiŋ hé uŋglúpi kiŋ.
- *I am eating baked bread.*

---

624. štéčhiya — *reserved* — Used to describe something or - someone that is reserved or kept apart from others.
• Wíčȟoškala štéčhiyapi kte lo.
- *He is reserved and quiet.*

---

625. owíŋyakA — *tidy* — Used to describe something that is neat, orderly, and well-organized.
• Háŋ owíŋyakA yé□l tA.
- *My room is tidy.*

---

626. úŋ — *combined* — Used to describe things that are combined or mixed together in the Lakota language. It implies a sense of unity or blending of different elements.
• Wíŋyaŋ šni áŋ úŋ osíčéčaŋkičiye.
- *The girls are wearing a combined dress.*

---

627. iwóktañi — *naval* — The word 'iwóktañi' is used to describe something related to the naval or belly button area.
• Wóktañišni čhákmuŋpi kiŋ čha hí iwóktañi táku.
- *He has a small tattoo near his naval.*

---

628. híŋhaŋ kísuyapi — *diving* — The term 'híŋhaŋ kísuyapi' in Lakota means 'diving'. It is used to describe the action of diving into water.
• Waníyetu kiŋ híŋhaŋ kísuyapi yeló.
- *I want to go diving in the winter.*

---

629. lila wówašte — *marvellous* — Used to describe something as marvellous or wonderful. It emphasizes the extraordinary nature or quality of the noun it is describing.

- Wíyakalika lila wówašte kiŋ hená okíčhize.
- *The sunset was truly marvellous yesterday.*

630. čhókaŋ kte — *banned* — The Lakota adjective 'čhókaŋ-kte' means 'banned' in English. It describes something that is prohibited or forbidden.
- Wíčhuŋčhikčupi kiŋ čhókaŋ kte.
- *I am banned from the store.*

631. háŋpaŋ — *jammed* — Used to describe something that is jammed or stuck in a fixed position.
- Máza háŋpaŋ tȟáŋka čha.
- *The door is jammed shut.*

632. oyáte wiwóŋspe — *democratic* — The adjective 'oyáte wiwóŋspe' in Lakota refers to something being 'democratic', meaning it is related to or characteristic of democracy. It describes a system of government in which power is held by the people.
- Héčhel iyoheyaŋkiŋ, oyáte wiwóŋspe kiŋ čhaŋté tuktíče kiŋlá.
- *In a good society, everyone has a say in the democratic decisions.*

633. ékŭŋškaŋ — *thoroughly* — The Lakota adjective 'ékŭŋškaŋ' means 'thoroughly' and is used to emphasize the completeness or detailed nature of an action or state.
- Wíŋyaŋ 'ékŭŋškaŋ' iyéča kte lo.
- *She cleaned the house 'thoroughly'.*

634. wíyuke — *antique* — Used to describe something as antique, meaning it is typically old-fashioned, out of date, or often of historical or cultural value.
- Hé waníyetu wíyuke kiŋ makȟá, héčhapi yelo.
- *This antique clock is very valuable, do not touch it.*

635. íŋyaŋmA — *nude* — Used to describe something or someone as being nude or without clothing.
- Háŋ, wóuŋspe íŋyaŋmA wóuŋspe.
- *Yes, the man is nude.*

636. oíya — *muttering* — Used to describe the act of muttering, speaking softly or quietly in a way that is difficult to hear or understand.
- Wíyakâta oíyawa kiŋ lenápi na iyélišni.
- *The man muttered something to his friend.*

637. wičhównA — *artistic* — Used to describe something or someone that is artistic or has artistic qualities.
- Héčhá wíčhównA kiŋ
- *She is very artistic*

638. okáhiŋze — *stray* — The Lakota term 'okáhiŋze' is used to describe something or someone that is wandering away from its normal path or location.
- Wíyanke okáhiŋze kiŋ čháŋté, hečéličupi kšté.
- *The stray dog found its way back home.*

639. wašákA — *sufficient* — Used to convey the idea of having enough or being sufficient in a particular context. It denotes a satisfactory quantity or quality of something.
- WíyakA wašákA kiŋ lápi kin hÀŠkA wì yákA.
- *I have sufficient food to make dinner.*

640. kókipA — *swinging* — Used to describe something that is swinging or in motion back and forth.
- Wóketu kókipA he? Héčhel tȟománi yeló!
- *Is that tree swinging? It looks so peaceful!*

641. wóyukiŋyaŋ — *intellectual* — Used to describe someone who is intelligent, knowledgeable, or possessing intellectual abilities.
- He is a wóyukiŋyaŋ person who always excels in his studies.
- *Thiwáhe tókaheya wóyukiŋyaŋ yelo, hečhetu kiŋ etáŋhaŋpi kte kale.*

642. išiyečiŋ — *wired* — Used to describe someone who is feeling wired or jittery due to heightened excitement or anxiety.
- Tokážu kiŋ išiyečiŋ yelo. Waníyetu kiŋ yečháŋ hén.
- *I am feeling wired today. I have a lot of energy.*

643. wákpA — *rapid* — Used to describe something that is moving or happening quickly or with great speed.
- WákpA olówačhiyA kiŋ hÉca kte.
- *The horse is running rapidly.*

644. čuŋwíŋyakA — *acceptable* — Used to express something that is deemed as acceptable or okay by a person or a group.
- Hečhel kiŋ lo čuŋwíŋyakA.
- *This food is acceptable.*

645. wičhála — *classy* — Used to describe someone or something as classy, elegant, or stylish.
- Wíčhaŋla wičhála kiŋ hí yuȟáŋpi.
- *She is very classy and sophisticated.*

646. tošpána — *bananas* — Used to describe something that is like a banana or has the characteristics of a banana.
- Iyéčhel uŋsí tošpána kiŋ čhaŋsála úŋ pȟaháblun héčhel.
- *These bananas are very tasty and healthy.*

647. olákič'iyA — *epic* — The word 'olákič'iyA' is used to describe something as epic or grand in scale.

• Háŋ mitákuyepi kte lo, héčhel olákič'iyA kiŋ čha.
- *We celebrated together, and it was truly an epic feast.*

---

648. ič'íčhib — *wont* — The word 'ič'íčhib' is used to describe something that is not likely or inclined to happen.
• Wíyayekiya kiŋ ič'íčhib kiŋ čhaŋkpé.
- *He won't come tomorrow.*

---

649. kéye — *thorough* — Used to describe something that is done very thoroughly, without cutting corners or missing any - details.
• WíkiyA kiyAblA ke
- *I washed the dishes thoroughly*

---

650. wówačhiŋyaka — *heroic* — Used to describe someone who is brave, courageous, and acts heroically in difficult situations.
• Heȟákta wówačhiŋyaka kiŋ, hé tȟawá niáče na kte.
- *He is a heroic warrior, always willing to help.*

---

651. íŋmamA — *chewing* — Used to describe the action of chewing or the state of being chewed.
• Wíyute yuŋ íŋmamA sni kte lo.
- *The dog is chewing on a bone.*

---

652. ómazAŋ — *atomic* — Used to describe something as atomic or related to atoms.
• Iyéčhel owíčhakiya ómazAŋ kiŋ hékta kiŋ.
- *The atomic bomb is very powerful.*

---

653. oieyapi — *cosmic* — The Lakota adjective 'oieyapi' is typically used to describe something that is related to the universe or cosmos. It conveys a sense of vastness, interconnectedness, and spirituality.

• Wakantanka ki le oyasin oieyapi kici omniciye.
- *God created all things cosmic and holy.*

---

654. úŋkík'A — *increasing* — The word 'úŋkíkA' is used to d-escribe something that is getting larger, growing, or becoming more abundant.
• Wakáŋ Táŋka úŋkík'A héčhel.
- *The Great Spirit is increasing in power.*

---

655. čháŋtóhphüska — *cheerful* — Used to describe someone or something that is cheerful and happy.
• Wičháša čháŋtóhphüska kiŋ hečhel.
- *The man is cheerful today.*

---

656. ičhómni — *sincerely* — This word is used to express genu-ine and heartfelt sincerity in communication or actions.
• WíyayAhe, kiŋ láwíčhómni kiŋ yáŋ ni.
- *Thank you, I sincerely appreciate it.*

---

657. iškáŋ — *whipped* — Used to describe something that has been whipped, beaten, or lashed.
• Wí yuȟá iškáŋ na hétuŋzape.
- *He is whipped because he was disobedient.*

---

658. wópičhinhna — *discreet* — The Lakota adjective 'wópičh-inhna' means discreet, being careful not to draw attention to oneself or one's actions.
• Waúŋšila wópičhinhnawičha kiŋ héčhel.
- *He is very discreet in his behavior.*

---

659. oowótȟuŋ — *surgical* — Used to describe something as being surgical or relating to surgery.
• Wíyuke-wíčhíyayečhapi kiŋ 'oowótȟuŋ' yuha t'óla kiŋ kte.
- *The doctor performed a 'surgical' procedure on the patient.*

660. itȟúŋkaŋ — *dental* — Used to describe anything related to the teeth or dental matters.
- Wíčeča itȟúŋkaŋ na wópila kiŋ čha líla.
- *The dentist helped fix my dental problems.*

661. wówičak'iye — *righteous* — The Lakota adjective 'wówičak'iye' means 'righteous' and describes someone who is morally upright or virtuous.
- Wówičak'iye oblaye kiŋ le, hečhel sluha yo.
- *The righteous man helps others.*

662. eyiíniyaŋyaŋ — *lively* — The Lakota adjective 'eyiíniyaŋyaŋ' describes something or someone as lively, full of energy and enthusiasm.
- Háŋ eyiíniyaŋyaŋ kiŋ yelo!
- *The children are very lively today!*

663. owápi wakȟáŋ — *virtually* — Used to convey the meaning of 'virtually' or 'almost'. It is used to indicate that something is very close to being completely true or accurate.
- He was owápi wakȟáŋ able to finish the project on time.
- *Wóuŋspe owápi wakȟáŋ eyásla kičhíčiyayapi kta.*

664. wašte yútA — *spicy* — The word 'wašte yútA' is used to describe food that has a spicy flavor or taste.
- Iyápi wašte yútA kičhí glí
- *The chili is very spicy*

665. wakíŋhdiyaŋ — *aged* — Used to describe something or someone as aged or old.
- Čhaŋté wakíŋhdiyaŋ yeló.
- *The horse is very aged.*

666. wíŋyakA — *preferred* — Used to describe something that is preferred or favored by someone.
● WíŋyakA kte lila oíyokA yelo.
- *I prefer to eat vegetables.*

667. ížaskaŋ — *superb* — The word 'ížaskaŋ' is used to describe something as being exceptional or excellent.
● Tokel ížaskaŋ na itážiŋ kiŋ híŋhaŋniya kiŋ.
- *The food is superb at this restaurant.*

668. oíyoǧeya — *sheer* — Used to describe something that is completely pure or undiluted, often used to emphasize the intensity or extremeness of a quality.
● Wíyokiyeya oíyoǧeya kiŋ, waníyetu wóglakapi kte lo.
- *The water is sheer pure, she just drank from the river.*

669. wíčhoka — *rational* — The Lakota adjective 'wíčhoka' means 'rational', referring to the ability to think or act logically and sensibly.
● Wíčhoka kiŋ làkollo he.
- *He always makes rational decisions.*

670. wówičhakA — *definite* — Used to indicate something that is definite or certain.
● HečhíŋkiyA wówičhakA kiŋ líla yAzá wóuŋspe tāku ye.
- *I am sure that she will come tomorrow.*

671. owíŋkčheča — *infinite* — The Lakota adjective 'owíŋkčheča' expresses the concept of something being without limits or endless.
● Tȟaté wóuŋspe owíŋkčheča kičhiyúsni tȟaŋíyayapi
- *The universe is infinitely vast and mysterious*

672. úŋzAŋ — *entertaining* — Used to describe something that is entertaining, enjoyable, or amusing.

● WíčhuŋzAŋ kiŋ hoká apižapi.

- *The movie is very entertaining.*

673. čhiŋkásaŋ — *realistic* — The Lakota adjective 'čhiŋkásaŋ' means 'realistic'. It is used to describe something that is based on practicality or reality rather than idealism or fantasy.

● Waúŋšila čhokíčiyapi kte, iyápi waštéya čhiŋkásaŋ naíŋžiču.

- *When making a plan, it is important to be realistic.*

674. woíci — *noted* — The Lakota adjective 'woíci' is used when something has been observed, acknowledged or recognized as important or significant.

● Wóiyayel owóyašničiyape, šničiyape kte ló.

- *I noted the important information that you gave me.*

675. wówičhikaŋ — *echoing* — The word 'wówičhikaŋ' is used to describe something that has an echoing sound or effect.

● Wówičhikaŋ čhaŋté wóuŋspe hé toŋ

- *The echoing laughter filled the canyon.*

676. waȟéčhe — *restored* — Used to describe something that has been brought back to its original state or condition.

● Híȟa waȟéčhe kiŋ hená áyazapȟelo.

- *The house has been restored after the storm.*

677. lila — *greatly* — Used to emphasize the degree or extent of something, indicating a high level of greatness or importance.

● Wakan Tanka omani lila kin.

- *The Great Spirit is truly important.*

678. owíŋyaŋ — *striking* — Used to describe something that is striking or noticeable in appearance or effect.

- Hé níkun niwíčhuŋka owíŋyaŋ čhaŋmúŋ kiŋ.
- *I saw a striking bird in the sky.*

---

679. uŋpičhiyA — *associated* — Used to describe something that is connected or related to something else.
- Thi hčhokinyA uŋpičhiyA ye.
- *This book is associated with that one.*

---

680. owákičhiyA — *purely* — The Lakota adjective 'owákičhiyA' refers to something that is pure or completely unadulterated.
- WíyayA owákičhiyA kté tohe.
- *He ate the food purely.*

---

681. ičupi — *ruling* — The word 'ičupi' is used to describe something or someone who has authority or control over others.
- Tuŋkášila wouníčupi kiŋ ló.
- *The chief is ruling the village.*

---

682. násape — *immune* — Used to describe something or someone that is immune to a certain disease or illness.
- Wíčhaša násape kiŋ ló.
- *The child is immune to smallpox.*

---

683. éčul — *utter* — Used to convey a sense of complete or extreme quality, emphasizing the full extent of something.
- Wíčhaša éčul kiŋ čhokápi kta tóka.
- *The man uttered a loud scream.*

---

684. ožáŋžaŋ — *authentic* — The Lakota term 'ožáŋžaŋ' is used to describe something that is genuine, real, or authentic.
- Waúŋšila kiŋ 'ožáŋžaŋ' nakúŋpi kte lo.
- *I appreciate their 'authentic' approach to this project.*

---

685. wíyuskaŋ — *elderly* — Used to describe someone who is elderly or advanced in age.
- Tȟókáhe wíyuskaŋ híŋbla oká kiŋ
- *The elderly man walks slowly*

---

686. čháŋzi — *gradually* — Used to describe a gradual or slow process. It implies that something is happening little by little over time.
- Wókičhupi čháŋzi kiŋ hená uŋžíyaka.
- *The plant is growing gradually under the sun.*

---

687. owápi — *fundamental* — Used to describe something that is essential or foundational to a concept or idea.
- Wíčhuȟčala owápi kiŋ là wapȟáŋ čha unyápi kiŋ.
- *The fire is a fundamental element of the Lakota way of life.*

---

688. wóowaza — *cunning* — The adjective wóowaza is used to describe someone who is clever, sly, or crafty in their actions.
- Wóowaza kiŋ ló!
- *He is very cunning!*

---

689. wačiŋčiŋyáŋ — *sounding* — Used to describe something that makes a sound. It is commonly used to describe objects or animals that produce noise.
- Šúŋkawakȟá chí kiŋ é wačiŋčiŋyáŋ yé.
- *The dogs are making a lot of noise.*

---

690. wókAšila — *snarling* — Used to describe something that is snarling or showing aggressive behavior.
- The wókAšila dog bared its teeth at the stranger.
- *Kíkta wókAšila pte snáke čháŋ wakȟáŋčiŋ kiŋ léčhiyaka.*

---

691. iyáŋžila — *upbeat* — The word 'iyáŋžila' is used to describe someone or something that is cheerful and positive in attit-

ude.
- Wičháša iyáŋžila kiŋ lená wokála.
- *The young man is always upbeat.*

692. ičhéčhaŋ — *select* — Used to describe something that has been carefully chosen or selected.
- Wíčhiče thíla khéya uŋyáŋpi kiŋ héčhaŋpi.
- *I chose the best apple from the selection.*

693. oyéče — *overboard* — Used to describe something going overboard or being excessive.
- Iyápi kte lo oyéče kiŋ táku śni.
- *He spent way too much money on that.*

694. wičhówašte — *temporarily* — Used to describe something that is only going to last for a short period of time or temporarily.
- Iyéchel wičhówašte šni wóptekiya.
- *I will be temporarily staying here.*

695. oyúspaŋ — *cozy* — Used to describe a feeling of warmth and comfort, often in a small or intimate space.
- Wíyaye kiŋ lená ómakȟa kiŋ keyá oyúspaŋ.
- *I love sitting by the fireplace because it is cozy.*

696. wówighta — *authorized* — Used to describe something that is authorized or allowed.
- Iyápi kta wówighta kiŋ lená otúhiyélo.
- *I am authorized to use this computer.*

697. wičhóhaŋ — *regularly* — Used to describe something that occurs regularly or consistently.
- Wašté wičhóhaŋ owíčhupi kiŋ čha oháŋ.
- *He always helps his neighbors.*

698. wičhíyakA — *competitive* — Used to describe something or someone who is competitive, striving to do better than others.
- Wóuŋspe wičhíyakA kiŋ héhaŋ.
- *He is very competitive when playing games.*

699. owíčhoŋ — *specially* — Used to describe something that is done in a special or particular way.
- Wíyakaspe kiŋ 'owíčhoŋ' kte.
- *They made it 'specially' for you.*

700. iwičhoŋ — *elementary* — The Lakota term 'iwičhoŋ' is used to describe something that is basic or fundamental, typically referring to elementary concepts or principles.
- Ožála iwičhoŋ kiŋ, okáȟčala kiŋyaiyayapi kte.
- *He is learning elementary math at school.*

701. wičhín — *hunted* — Used to describe something that has been hunted, indicating that it is the object of a hunt.
- 'Wičhín kiŋ he? Wičhíŋčeye kiŋ he?'
- *Is it hunted? Is it already hunted?*

702. owáŋyaŋ — *partial* — When using 'owáŋyaŋ', you are describing something as being incomplete or not full.
- Ičháškapi kiŋ, tókahe owáŋyaŋ tókahe kiŋ hé.
- *In the cup, there is a partially filled cup.*

703. owóŋspeyayA — *neutral* — Used to describe something or someone as neutral, unbiased, or impartial.
- Wíyakesni wašíču owóŋspeyayA kiŋ lenábla he.
- *The judge remained neutral in the case.*

704. wíye — *carved* — Used to describe something that has been carved or sculpted.

● Wíye kiŋ hena thípi ká uŋkičiŋ hé ómahan.

- *The carved tree stands tall and proud.*

---

705. wičhak'iye — *psychiatric* — Used to describe something related to psychiatry or mental health.

● Héčhel kiŋ dakhóta wičhak'iye tawáčhel uŋspéič kiŋ.

- *He decided to seek psychiatric help.*

---

706. awéwotapi iyečhiŋ — *weekly* — Used to describe something that occurs or is done once a week.

● Iyéthuŋpi kiŋ yútapi awéwotapi iyečhiŋ.

- *I go to the gym weekly.*

---

707. ičiŋkbyA — *extended* — The word 'ičiŋkbyA' is used to describe something that is extended or stretched out in length.

● Wí isakpe kiŋ wičhášta kiŋ waŋná wasíču, úŋwačhá abyA.

- *The snake crawled across the field, its body extended.*

---

708. háškaŋ — *curly* — Used to describe something that is curly in nature, such as hair or a spiral shape.

● Nážiŋ háškaŋ yelo.

- *Her hair is curly.*

---

709. iŋžáŋžiŋ — *solitary* — Used to describe something or someone as being solitary or alone.

● Wíyakwitaŋ héčhel uŋčíktelo iŋžáŋžiŋ.

- *The wolf prefers to be solitary.*

---

710. oyáte wačhíŋ — *environmental* — The term 'oyáte wačhíŋ' is used to describe something that is related to the environment or natural surroundings.

• Mní wičhóni kte lo. Oyáte wačhíŋ eyápi.
- *The water is contaminated. It is an environmental issue.*

---

711. ičhóhotapi — *elaborate* — Used to describe something that is detailed, thorough, or intricate. It is used to refer to something that has been carefully thought out and clearly explained.
• He įčhóhotapi kiŋ lila thípi kiŋ, owáyawa kiŋ šká.
- *She did an elaborate job of decorating the house.*

---

712. iwásaŋ — *gifted* — The Lakota term 'iwásaŋ' is used to describe someone who has been given a gift or talent, often in the context of spiritual or natural abilities.
• Wičháčhiyaye kiŋ iwásaŋyelo pi.
- *He is a very gifted speaker.*

---

713. owóčhichiyA — *stoned* — Used to describe something or someone as being stoned or under the influence of drugs or alcohol.
• Wíčhawo owóčhichiyA kiŋ
- *The man is stoned.*

---

714. čháŋpi wičhówašte — *diplomatic* — The term 'čháŋpi wičhówašte' in Lakota refers to being skilled in dealing with others in a tactful and sensitive way to avoid conflict.
• Wíčhaša kiŋ čháŋpi wičhówašte kiŋ he?
- *Is that man diplomatic?*

---

715. wičhówičakaŋ — *successfully* — Used to describe an action or task that has been completed or achieved successfully.
• Wana wíčhówičakaŋ kiŋ heháŋpi.
- *He/she did the work successfully.*

---

716. akíčhupi — *acquired* — Used to describe something that has been obtained or gained through effort or a process.

• Wí can aglápi kiŋ lená wóglakati, akíčhupi kuwé.
- *I worked hard to get this car, it was acquired.*

717. wóčhuŋkiyaŋ — *audio* — The word 'wóčhuŋkiyaŋ' is used to describe something related to sound or audio.
• Wóčhuŋkiyaŋ na elk eyápa kiŋ hé.
- *The audio of the elk is beautiful.*

718. khukhúš — *swift* — Used to describe something that is fast or quick in movement.
• Waníyetu khukhúšlá, wíyópe lo.
- *The winter is swift, the days are short.*

719. waŋgláke — *programmed* — The Lakota adjective 'waŋgláke' means 'programmed' and is used to describe something that has been set with a specific plan or system in mind.
• Wičhákta waŋgláke kiŋ uŋgíyapi kte lo.
- *The computer is programmed to turn off by itself.*

720. wíyam — *colored* — Used to describe something as having a color or being colored.
• Wíyam lila waste sni.
- *The dress is colored blue.*

721. owáŋžila — *invincible* — The Lakota adjective 'owáŋžila' describes something or someone that is impossible to defeat or overcome.
• He is known for his owáŋžila strength and determination.
- *Héčhel šniye owáŋžila ičhápi hé.*

722. wakȟáŋžiče — *civilized* — Used to describe something or someone as civilized in a manner that reflects a level of sophistication, refinement, and adherence to social norms.

• Hečáka wakȟáŋžiče kiŋ aȟčháŋ čhaŋtéwaŋ kté.
- *The city is considered civilized by many people.*

---

723. waŋkátu — *peacefully* — Used to describe something happening in a peaceful manner or state.
• Wamakȟáȟni waŋkátu kin héčha.
- *She sleeps peacefully.*

---

724. wóuŋspekhiya — *employed* — Used to describe someone who is currently working or employed.
• Wóuŋspekhiya le hčhokuye kiŋ kte, le yuhapi kiŋ eyazan kiŋ hi.
- *He is employed at the store, so he is able to provide for his family.*

---

725. naye — *detected* — Used to describe something that has been detected or found.
• Wakhinyan ki naye.
- *He found the lost horse.*

---

726. tháŋka — *roughly* — Used to describe something that is roughly or approximately a certain way.
• Iyápi tháŋka kiŋ lá.
- *The distance is roughly two miles.*

---

727. čhóni šké — *surprisingly* — Used to describe something that is unexpected or surprising.
• Wíčhaša wašté čhóni šké kiŋ he waŋžíya.
- *The man was surprisingly happy when he saw the sunrise.*

---

728. iyúha ale — *daring* — The word 'iyúha ale' means 'daring' and is used to describe someone who is bold and courageous in their actions or decisions.
• Wétanye iyúha ale kiŋ héhaŋni.
- *He is very daring in his hunting.*

---

729. wakšíčhala — *celebrated* — Used to describe something that is celebrated or revered.
● Čhaŋtéšni na kte wíyaka wakšíčhala kiŋ čhaŋlíla tuka hé nakúŋ.
- *The people celebrated the birth of their new leader with a great feast.*

---

730. hiŋháŋla — *eldest* — Used to describe the eldest or oldest member of a group or family.
● Háŋ mitákuye oyás'iŋ, hiŋháŋla wanyétuŋka emáčiya.
- *In my extended family, my eldest brother is a police officer.*

---

731. pȟéthuŋ — *juvenile* — The word 'pȟéthuŋ' is used to describe something as being juvenile or immature.
● Wíyawapȟe wayawa kiŋ
- *The young horse is playful.*

---

732. sápA — *slippery* — Used to describe something that is slippery or difficult to grip.
● WíyAkiyA sápA le.
- *The road is slippery.*

---

733. mnihúŋka — *parallel* — Used to describe things that are parallel to each other, meaning they are always the same distance apart and will never meet.
● Iyé mnihúŋkapi kta éya uŋ thkítuŋ mnaŋ
- *The two roads are parallel to each other*

---

734. owákhiphičhA — *exceptional* — Used to describe something as exceptional or extraordinary in Lakota language.
● Héčhekšičíla owákhiphičhA kiŋ hÉya WíčhAšA Kiŋ, kičhíyA.
- *The sunset was exceptional in the Badlands, it was beautiful.*

---

735. thókȟuŋkA — *presidential* — Used to describe something or someone as 'presidential', indicating qualities or characterist-

ics associated with the president.
- Ťhaté thókȟuŋkA kiŋ he ášikicu,
- *The chief acts like a president, but there is no salary.*

---

736. waníyetuštala — *potentially* — Used to indicate some-thing that has the possibility or capability of happening in the future.
- Hékta waníyetuštala kičhiyāpi yuhá unčhíyaya.
- *The storm could potentially arrive tomorrow.*

---

737. thókA — *numerous* — Used to describe something that is plentiful in quantity or many in number.
- WíyakA thókA tháblAka kiŋ lé oíyAkičhiyA.
- *There are numerous flowers in the garden.*

---

738. akíču — *automatically* — Used to describe something that happens automatically or without conscious thought or effort.
- Waúŋšila akíču kiŋ hí.
- *The sun rises automatically.*

---

739. háŋska ečhél — *freaky* — Used to describe something - that is strange, weird or out of the ordinary, often in a negative connotation.
- Wakȟáŋ héčha kiŋ, háŋska ečhél kiŋ.
- *The thunderstorm is coming, it's going to be freaky.*

---

740. khéŋ — *hotter* — Used to describe something as hotter than another temperature or object.
- Wíyuke tháŋka khéŋ. He kiŋ lé hótèl.
- *The coffee is hotter. Than the hotel.*

---

741. waŋžíčhA — *sane* — Used to describe someone who is mentally stable and rational.

- WíyakA waŋžíchA kiŋ hečhá
- *He seems to be very sane.*

742. sáŋmóŋhaya — *worldwide* — Used to describe something that is found, known, or happening all over the world.
- Ťho sáŋmóŋhaya čhaŋtéyapi kte, ťhawášničaye yo.
- *They speak a worldwide language, English.*

743. kȟepA — *melted* — Used to describe something that has turned from solid to liquid due to heating or warmth.
- Lé za kȟepA kuwá!
- *The snow has melted!*

744. wóčhekiya — *apparent* — Used to describe something that is clearly visible or obvious.
- Tokáhe kiŋ čhokápi wóčhekiya.
- *The car accident was apparent.*

745. tokáhe — *newly* — Used to describe something that is newly formed, created, or acquired.
- Wí tokáhe unkíyapi kiŋ kte.
- *I bought a new shirt.*

746. thóžA — *smashing* — Used to describe something as 'smashing'. It can be used to indicate that something is excellent, impressive, or outstanding.
- Hímani kiŋ thóžA hečhá uŋ wíčha kiŋ.
- *They have a smashing house.*

747. thíkičhiyaŋ — *valid* — The Lakota term 'thíkičhiyaŋ' is used to describe something as valid or acceptable.
- Hečhé kiŋ thíkičhiyaŋ ní!
- *Is this valid?*

748. čhą — *juicy* — The Lakota adjective 'čhą' means 'juicy' and is used to describe fruits or other foods that are moist and full of liquid. It emphasizes the freshness and succulence of the food.
- Wí ní čhą gláža kiŋ mázi.
- *This apple is very juicy.*

749. ičhékhiphičheya — *tactical* — Used to describe something that is related to strategy or tactics, particularly in a military context.
- Wíčhaša kiŋ okípapi hečéšiča kiŋ hečháblapi tawóiyaye kiŋ ké kta
- *The warrior made a tactical decision in order to win the battle.*

750. ųží — *repeated* — The word 'ųží' is used to indicate something that is repeated or done more than once.
- Wóžupi kte átaŋhaŋ čháŋkúŋkiyapi wóžupi šni.
- *He told the same story a second time.*

751. mošpó — *ashore* — The word 'mošpó' is used to describe something or someone being on the shore or by the water's edge.
- WíyakA tAka ye mošpó.
- *The boat is ashore.*

752. wapȟé — *drugged* — Used to describe something or someone as 'drugged' or under the influence of drugs.
- Nážuȟa nakun 'wapȟé'.
- *He looks drugged.*

753. iňtáŋ — *dynamic* — Used to describe something or someone as dynamic, active, or full of energy.
- Wíčháša waŋ iňtáŋ kiŋ čhaŋté.
- *The young man is very dynamic.*

754. iyúspe — *shaped* — Used to describe the shape of an object or person, indicating that it is formed in a specific way.
- Wíyakȟemni iyúspe kiŋ uŋglonápi kte.
- *The house is shaped like a rectangle.*

755. owákitahe — *warmer* — Used to describe something that is warmer than something else. It can be used to compare temperatures, weather, or objects that produce heat.
- Nahé thiyóȟeyelo wowáyake owákitahe.
- *Today is warmer than yesterday.*

756. nupȟá — *mute* — The word 'nupȟá' is used to describe someone who is unable to speak or communicate verbally.
- Wí?iyayá nupȟápi kiŋ, níyé.
- *The child is mute, he cannot speak.*

757. owíyuspa — *understandable* — The word 'owíyuspa' is used to describe something that is easy to comprehend or make sense of.
- Unkí yeló! Thíyospaye owíyuspa hé!
- *Come here! The instructions are understandable!*

758. iŋkȟáŋ — *secondary* — Used to describe something as being secondary or of lesser importance compared to something else.
- Hečétu iŋkȟáŋ kiŋ lákota kiŋ.
- *English is a secondary language to Lakota.*

759. mažó — *wrecked* — Used to describe something as being wrecked or destroyed. It is often used to refer to physical objects that are damaged beyond repair.
- Wíyayič'iyapi mažó owíčhel wópila kiŋ láŋhapéya.
- *The car is completely wrecked and cannot be driven.*

760. iŋčhéyeya — *ripe* — Used to describe something that is ripe or mature, typically referring to fruits or vegetables that are ready to be eaten.
● Wanbli iŋčhéyeya kiŋ lená Flower Cheese
- *The apple is ripe and ready to be picked.*

---

761. ič'íŋyaŋ — *collective* — Used to describe a group or collection of things or people.
● Hokšíla čhaškápaye iyéič'íŋyaŋ kiŋ hečápi kiŋ hokšíla po.
- *The children collected a large amount of firewood and now they are playing.*

---

762. eškúŋ — *motherfucking* — The adjective 'eškúŋ' is used in Lakota language to express intensity or emphasis. It is often used as a strong curse word similar to 'motherfucking' in English.
● šni Iyéšica eškúŋ héčhena.
- *That motherfucking dog is always barking.*

---

763. ičá — *commanding* — The word 'ičá' means 'commanding', used to describe someone or something that possesses authority or power.
● 'Hówa, kiŋ lá čha wóglakiyeyapi, kiŋ hena šni keyčékupi.', kiŋ un wicála kiŋ.
- *Wait, if you don't follow the rules, you will face consequences, as I am the one in charge.*

---

764. uŋkíčheya — *ernest* — The word 'uŋkíčheya' means 'ernest', describing someone who is serious, sincere, and committed.
● Wíyaka uŋkíčheya kiŋ Kȟaŋže; yeló wótȟeya Glíčhokapi.
- *Ernest is a very serious person; he always keeps his promises.*

---

765. itonáŋye — *polar* — Used to describe something or someone as polar, relating to the regions located around the North and South poles.

- Wíčhaša wakpána itonáŋye yelo.
- *The man swims in the polar water.*

---

766. owáŋičeya — *merciful* — Used to describe someone who shows compassion and forgiveness towards others in a kind and generous manner.
- Wakȟáŋyežapi kiŋ owáŋičeya ye.
- *He is very merciful.*

---

767. owaníyeka — *supportive* — Owaníyeka means 'supportive-' in Lakota. It describes someone who provides assistance and encouragement to others.
- Waníyetu wasté owaníyeka kiŋ lená hékta
- *My best friend is very supportive*

---

768. okíčhizečhepi — *medieval* — The Lakota adjective 'okíčhizečhepi' means 'medieval'. It describes something that is related to or characteristic of the Middle Ages, a period in European history from the 5th to the 15th century.
- Wókige okíčhizečhepi kiŋ láǧe yelo.
- *This castle looks medieval.*

---

769. uŋmákičheyan — *unarmed* — The Lakota adjective 'uŋmákičheyan' means 'unarmed', referring to someone without weapons or defense.
- Wakíŋyan na uŋmákičheyan kiŋ lé lená wíŋyaŋpi.
- *The woman felt vulnerable because she was unarmed.*

---

770. owáŋčaŋ — *historic* — The Lakota adjective 'owáŋčaŋ' means historic and is used to describe something that is related to the past or has significant historical importance.
- Tȟáŋka owáŋčaŋ kiŋ héčhokaŋpi kte lo, Thíthȟuŋwaŋ na héktaŋpi.
- *The historic buffalo hunt was a powerful event for the tribe.*

---

771. itóŋčhaŋ — *sonic* — Used to describe something related to sound or sound waves, usually in the context of being loud or powerful.
- Speakers produced a itóŋčhaŋ sound at the concert.
- *Parímawiŋyaŋpi kte lo, ečéla itóŋčhaŋ ólowaŋléča.*

---

772. oóyuŋkA — *homosexual* — Used to describe someone who is homosexual.
- Wíčhasa oóyuŋkA kiŋ hi, hečháktaŋpi kiŋ lúta pi, óme wayú kažútaŋpi kiŋ lúta pi.
- *The young man is homosexual, that's why he prefers to be with other men rather than women.*

---

773. itóŋkaŋ — *tropical* — Used to describe something as - tropical, typically referring to a climate or region with hot and humid weather.
- Wí yawé 'itóŋkaŋ' kiŋ lenápi kičhí tyáȟpi wóečháŋ.
- *We will vacation in a 'tropical' place next summer.*

---

774. wayákičheya — *glowing* — Used to describe something that is glowing or emitting light.
- Héčhel wayákičheya kiŋ
- *The fire is glowing brightly*

---

775. čhíŋsasa — *gigantic* — Used to describe something that is extremely large or huge.
- Čhíŋsasawapi kičhízapi kta čhíŋsasa kiŋ.
- *The elephant is truly gigantic.*

---

776. eháŋni — *moreover* — Used to add emphasis or provide additional information to a point that has already been made.
- Matȟó Thíkša, éya, eháŋni yeló.
- *The bear is strong and moreover smart.*

---

777. iyéčel — *positively* — Used to describe something in a positive manner. It is used to indicate a positive quality or characteristic of a person or thing.
- Waníyetu iyéčel kiŋ héčha.
- *Winter positively not is bad.*

778. wóičhake — *exquisite* — Used to describe something that is of exceptional beauty or high quality, something exquisite or marvelous.
- Wóičhake kičhíčeya šni.
- *You have an exquisite dress.*

779. iwá — *backstage* — Used to describe something that is behind the scenes or behind the main action, similar to the concept of being backstage in a theater or performance setting.
- Wíyukšá iyápi kiŋ hoká okɪlála. Wíyukšá yeló.
- *The real work is done behind the scenes. They are backstage.*

780. ičhiní — *vocal* — The word 'ičhiní' is used to describe something that is related to the voice or sound produced by speaking or singing.
- Wíyaka kiŋ 'ičhiní wíyaka kiŋ na wíyela.'
- *The bird sings a vocal song.*

781. thókA — *arctic* — Used to describe something as arctic or extremely cold.
- Uŋspéičič'iyabi wašté thókA.
- *The water in the lake is very arctic.*

782. akíčheya — *courageous* — The word 'akíčheya' is used to describe someone who shows bravery and fearlessness in the face of danger or adversity.
- Waníyetu akíčheya kiŋ lé, nížiŋ kiŋ níwíčaŋkte pi.
- *During the winter, he is courageous and never complains.*

783. wičhákte — *feminine* — Used to describe something that is feminine in nature or characteristics.

• Wičhákte wíyakȟa uŋ.

- *She is a feminine dancer.*

784. ičhémnaŋ — *slick* — Used to describe something smooth or slick, often in reference to a surface or object that is slippery or polished.

• Wíčhémnaŋ kȟéoyake.

- *The floor is slick.*

785. įži — *repeatedly* — Used to indicate that an action is done repeatedly or habitually.

• Wíyukšiča kte lo, héčen tȟáŋka čhaŋté įži.

- *Every morning, she drinks coffee repeatedly.*

786. čhúŋ — *butch* — Used to describe something or someone as 'butch'. It is often used to describe a person who displays traditionally masculine traits or behaviors.

• Nážiŋ wičhása kiŋ 'čhúŋ' héčha.

- *That man is very 'butch'.*

787. wišté — *partly* — Used to describe something that is partially or partly something else.

• Wílaxa šni, wišté yuya waúŋspe.

- *I can see it, but only partially clearly.*

788. wonášte — *monthly* — Used to describe something that occurs on a monthly basis or refers to a period of one month.

• Owáyawačupi kte lo, wonášte kiŋ kte ló.

- *I get paid monthly.*

789. wóyakhi — *likewise* — Used to indicate that something is similarly or in the same way as something else.

● Lila lúta kte wóyakhi.
- *She dances likewise.*

---

790. iŋŋótȟaŋ — *secondly* — Used to indicate the second item or action in a series of events or items.
● Wíčhaša waŋ iŋŋótȟaŋ kiŋ lóǧa tȟášniča kiŋ.
- *The man ate the second piece of meat.*

---

791. oyátekičhiyapi — *publicly* — Used to describe something that is done or happening in a public or open manner.
● Lakȟól'iyapi híŋkpagȟa, ožú kihíkta ilá wókiyaka. Oyátekičhi-yapi kštó.
- *We will have a meeting tomorrow, so make sure to spread the news. It will be done publicly.*

---

792. owákhičhA — *experimental* — Used to describe something that is experimental or in the process of being tested.
● Tokáha tȟókša owákhičhA kiŋ héčha.
- *The new medicine is experimental but promising.*

---

793. ičhépA — *relaxing* — The word 'ičhépA' is used to describe something that brings feelings of relaxation or calmness.
● Wíyute kiŋ le úŋčíč'éla, waníyetu kte lo. Wóičhič'éla.
- *If you are tired, take a break. It is relaxing.*

---

794. ičhmúŋke — *openly* — Used to describe something that is done or expressed in a way that is open or without reserve.
● Wíčhaša waŋ ičhmúŋke kiŋ hečízapi kte.
- *The man spoke openly about his feelings.*

---

795. oóyuŋke — *liberal* — The Lakota adjective 'oóyuŋke' means 'liberal' and describes someone who is generous or open-minded, willing to give freely without expecting anything in return.

- He is known for his oóyuŋke nature, always sharing what he has with others.
- *Wówapi kin lila oóyuŋke yelo, hehal iyéya unkúwaŋpi kin lená.*

---

796. oíčhíŋla — *guarded* — Used to describe something or - someone that is protected or watched carefully.
- Héčha oíčhíŋla le, he is a guarded man.
- *He is watched carefully.*

---

797. ičhíŋčhaŋwiyé — *briefly* — Used to describe something that is short in duration or concisely presented.
- Wičhíŋčhaŋwiyé kičhízapi kiŋ sni sni sni.
- *He told the story briefly.*

2. Index of Words

351. hačhá oyúsaza	dramatic
338. hačhá	specific
319. haŋká	latest
19. heháŋ	then
35. heya	still
4. heči	so
1. hiyá	no
96. hiŋ-néča	funny
422. hiŋ	hip
730. hiŋháŋla	eldest
211. hokšína	correct
569. hokšíče	freely
591. hoǧá	stinking
457. hoȟúŋ	faithful
44. háŋka	new
631. háŋpaŋ	jammed
739. háŋska ečhél	freaky
78. háŋska	far
436. háŋtaŋhaŋ	currently
39. háŋtokeca	after
708. háškaŋ	curly
7. hé	there
69. héhaŋ	ago
32. hékta	even
48. héčhe	ever
37. héčhetu	maybe
447. héčhu	traditional
628. híŋhaŋ kísuyapi	diving
174. híŋhaŋ	further
33. híŋhaŋna	sure
462. híŋtaŋ	fairly
142. hókšaŋ	anywhere

49. hók'ila	old
135. hówa	instead
433. icúšte	finest
560. ihékta	objective
619. ikčháŋ	continuing
145. imá, waŋká	interesting
132. imá	dark
593. ináźiŋ	demanding
603. ipá	printed
201. isnáȟna	blind
765. itonáŋye	polar
325. itztáŋ	sensitive
308. itáŋčhaŋyaŋ	international
773. itóŋkaŋ	tropical
771. itóŋčhaŋ	sonic
303. itȟáŋka	sometime
578. itȟóthi	subtle
660. itȟúŋkaŋ	dental
621. iwakhíhiyuŋ	accepting
700. iwičhoŋ	elementary
779. iwá	backstage
579. iwáhetena	magnetic
595. iwákin	stunning
712. iwásaŋ	gifted
233. iwáŋ	ancient
217. iwáŋyaŋkapi	nearly
456. iwéčȟuŋ	solo
577. iwízi	delightful
627. iwóktañi	naval
425. iye	abroad
405. iyohlogde	upper
254. iyÁ	familiar

27. iyápi	only
5. iyás'a	just
167. iyáya	usually
470. iyáŋ	remaining
691. iyáŋžila	upbeat
10. iyéna	up

506. iyétokčaŋ	maximum
477. iyéya	attacking
43. iyéyapi kiŋ	better
777. iyéčel	positively
485. iyéčetu	accidentally
466. iyéčhala	anonymous
190. iyéčheca	asleep
22. iyéčhetu	too
604. iyókihi	grounded
572. iyókiphi	emotionally
584. iyókiyapi	respectable
549. iyóku	mentally
407. iyókȟaŋ	happily
596. iyómakȟaŋ	exotic
448. iyómakȟiŋyaŋ	unconscious
368. iyópta	nearby
182. iyótake	indeed
102. iyótȟA	alright
115. iyówaŋšičA	lucky
616. iyówašte	universal
594. iyóyakapi	flowing
467. iyóyaŋ	operating
416. iyóyo	differently
570. iyóšiča	classical

728.	iyúha ale	daring
222.	iyúha	nowhere
754.	iyúspe	shaped
434.	iyútȟapi	softly
648.	ič'íčhib	wont
761.	ič'íŋyaŋ	collective
780.	ičhiní	vocal
794.	ičhmúŋke	openly
158.	ičhá	sleeping
581.	ičhániptȟapi	ambitious
343.	ičháŋ	touching
516.	ičháŋska	originally
283.	ičháŋčha	curious
749.	ičhékhiphičheya	tactical
784.	ičhémnaŋ	slick
793.	ičhépA	relaxing
692.	ičhéčhaŋ	select
140.	ičhíŋčhA	entire
797.	ičhíŋčhaŋwiyé	briefly
711.	ičhóhotapi	elaborate
656.	ičhómni	sincerely
707.	ičiŋkbyA	extended
681.	ičupi	ruling
763.	ičá	commanding
9.	ičámna	out
3.	ičíč'iyapi	all
753.	iňtáŋ	dynamic
758.	iŋkháŋ	secondary
432.	iŋyaŋ	inner
94.	iŋyékaŋ	outside
112.	iŋyétȟaŋka	fast
606.	iŋzí	incoming

760. inčhéyeya	ripe
790. inŋótȟaŋ	secondly
709. inžáŋžiŋ	solitary
642. išiyečiŋ	wired
657. iškáŋ	whipped
371. išniya	merely
47. išná	around
328. išnála	steady
357. ištanála	gentle
420. ištáwaye	shortly
24. ištáŋ	down
468. ištíma	visual
573. išáŋhna	visible
586. išáŋkhota	protective
150. ižáŋgúnaŋ	english
419. iȟápta	drawn
326. iȟúŋšičA	mobile
206. katé	knowing
526. kaŋ	horny
76. kağákapi	working
718. khukhúš	swift
551. khéčhiyela	rattling
740. khéŋ	hotter
116. kiktel	known
123. kiní	early
28. kipáhda	over
160. kiye	obviously
98. kičhíle	ahead
125. kičhízA	absolutely
525. kičúŋti	nearest
14. kiŋháŋ	as
539. kiŋháŋl	consistent

207.	koté	due
287.	ksá	wise
189.	kté	apparently
649.	kéye	thorough
517.	kíčiwičháŋ	sworn
488.	kíčiwíčhakča	electronic
502.	kíčíjašká	electrical
640.	kókipA	swinging
743.	kȟepA	melted
418.	kȟáŋ	catching
120.	kȟóla	straight
20.	k'iŋ	some

540.	lechel	awhile
11.	leháŋ	now
585.	lečháŋ	casual
442.	lgáŋ	shining
475.	lgáŋtaŋ	roaring
629.	lila wówašte	marvellous
677.	lila	greatly
6.	lé	here
246.	léčhaŋ	barely
66.	léčhetu	also
38.	mahé	before
438.	mahóta	vast
571.	makíkčiŋ	pressing
51.	makȟóčhe	every
482.	mat'éče	keen
178.	matȟó	low
107.	mayáŋke	perhaps
144.	mašíčA	fair

759. mažó	wrecked
244. miye	personally
575. mičhá	underwater
428. mni	marine
733. mnihúŋka	parallel
537. mní	fluid
751. mošpó	ashore
175. máku	upstairs
417. máni	global
146. máza	short
589. na!	instantly
337. nakúŋ	practically
725. naye	detected
99. niya-wakȟáŋ	living
583. niyúŋka	controlling
126. niá	moving
149. nišíčA	proud
756. nupȟá	mute
682. násape	immune
80. nážiŋ	anyway
56. nážiŋtku	else
220. nína wašté	super
464. níyuŋ	specifically
177. núŋpa	twice
461. ohʼáŋke	overnight
494. ohíye	bold
108. ohúŋ	back
653. oieyapi	cosmic
95. okȟáŋ	hot
605. oktáŋwaŋ	lined
638. okáhiŋze	stray
550. okáhni oíhanke	importantly

404.	okál'Owa	safely
118.	okážaŋ	somewhere
165.	okíkta	suddenly
212.	okíl	hardly
460.	okíle	humble
615.	okíyakapi	overseas
113.	okíyaŋ	finally
139.	okíčhiya	forever
198.	okíčhize	military
768.	okíčhizečhepi	medieval
166.	okíȟteŋ	immediately
608.	okšá	shattered
276.	okšíčha	central
306.	okȟá	leading
322.	okȟátA	bound
93.	okȟáte	sometimes
302.	okȟí	senior
374.	okȟóḣi	confident
531.	oltéwaye	logical
647.	olákič'iyA	epic
394.	oláŋpa	southern
249.	oláȟiŋ	obvious
409.	olówan	musical
183.	olówaŋ	empty
129.	ookíyapi	missing
659.	oowótȟuŋ	surgical
251.	opáwŋaŋ	foreign
258.	opáčuŋ	indistinct
301.	opáȟíŋ	alien
54.	opȟétȟuŋpi	own
566.	opȟéyatka	compound
437.	osnókiye	rising

545. ostéča	identical
253. oškáŋ	grown
285. ošmá	silent
284. ošnayaŋ	someday
245. ošnaye	sudden
243. ošni	hidden
496. otéwaye	formal
352. otȟaŋi	valuable
364. otȟúŋwaŋ	underground
767. owaníyeka	supportive
219. owaŋ	original
221. owaŋyákapi	truly
597. owašlí	fitting
237. owá	wet
568. owáekiyapi	beautifully
599. owáhiyeya	efficient
490. owájikale	blank
480. owákahni	significant

552. owákahŋ	sentimental
580. owákatuya	elite
734. owákhiphičhA	exceptional
792. owákhičhA	experimental
84. owákikiye	quite
755. owákitahe	warmer
680. owákičhiyA	purely
232. owákpamni	lately
622. owákte	improved
607. owáktomni	contained
291. owále	popular
367. owályaŋkapi	equal

360. owályaŋpi	basic
476. owápahmi	alternative
663. owápi wakȟáŋ	virtually
687. owápi	fundamental
36. owátanna	again
592. owáwašte	gracious
542. owáyakapi	cultural
612. owáyesica	thoughtful
598. owáyečin	gladly
83. owáčekiye	least
613. owáčhičhiyA	forensic
181. owáŋ	written
454. owáŋgaye	corporal
766. owáŋičeya	merciful
170. owáŋka	final
435. owáŋkaŋ	multiple
378. owáŋskeya	technically
400. owáŋspe	active
702. owáŋyaŋ	partial
193. owáŋye	famous
770. owáŋčaŋ	historic
721. owáŋžila	invincible
512. owášič'a	instrumental
231. owášte	handsome
42. owáštensica	last
478. owášteča	surprising
617. owášteče	supposedly
620. owáštečhila	advised
600. owášté	compromised
529. owíkič'aŋka	blaring
562. owíthukča	deliberately
514. owíyokiphi	economic

757. owíyuspa	understandable
240. owíċakiya	soft
491. owíċazi	glorious
587. owíčha	intent
522. owíčhakič'a	proven
515. owíčhak'a	loudly
547. owíčhathuŋ	industrial
699. owíčhoŋ	specially
671. owíŋkčheča	infinite
215. owíŋyahħa	powerful
625. owíŋyakA	tidy
678. owíŋyaŋ	striking
75. owíŋžala	second
623. owóthuŋ	baked
199. owówa	common
713. owóčhichiyA	stoned
703. owóŋspeyayA	neutral
200. owóšte	willing
710. oyáte wačhíŋ	environmental
632. oyáte wiwóŋspe	democratic
486. oyáte wówaši	pacific
105. oyáte	serious
791. oyátekičhiyapi	publicly
453. oyáwote	relative
259. oyáŋkA	carefully
62. oyétu	already
693. oyéče	overboard
695. oyúspaŋ	cozy
429. ozá	soviet
541. ozí	shiny
359. oákaŋke	officially
548. oíhimna	confidential

226.	oíhȟaye	dry
574.	oíke	outstanding
342.	oíkčakiyA	heavily
567.	oínažiŋ	supporting
403.	oíwakȟe	helpful
636.	oíya	muttering
401.	oíyayA	serial
68.	oíyok;atek	open
82.	oíyoketekiye	fun
327.	oíyokiphiye	joint
609.	oíyote	hereby
668.	oíyoǧeya	sheer
796.	oíčhíŋla	guarded
356.	oówaŋyaŋk	western
772.	oóyuŋkA	homosexual
795.	oóyuŋke	liberal
194.	očhíŋ	wild
684.	ožáŋžaŋ	authentic
273.	oȟáte	physical
263.	oȟáŋ	sexual
262.	oȟáŋke	tall
188.	oȟŋíŋ	warm
590.	phisíŋ	hairy
451.	phézi	broad

271.	piyá	healthy
340.	psíč	mysterious
731.	pȟéthuŋ	juvenile
164.	pȟó	fat
260.	sapsáčA	sexy
100.	ska	white

270. snuhe	pure
444. sní	unfair
307. soksáŋ	similar
269. stéya	clever
305. sťháŋkA	sharp
732. sápA	slippery
348. sápe	frankly
742. sáŋmóŋhaya	worldwide
161. sáŋni	slow
310. síću	alert
13. t'e	well
479. t'ó	tender
489. t'óče	bare
473. takú	primary
524. taŋhúškila	essential
527. taŋišila	ultimately
179. taŋyáŋ	awesome
133. taŋíčhA	totally
79. thiŋháŋ	inside
726. tháŋka	roughly
309. théȟówaŋka	federal
747. thíkičhiyaŋ	valid
40. thípi	home
173. thípiya	pregnant
781. thókA	arctic
735. thókȟuŋkA	presidential
746. thóžA	smashing
31. tkáyahaŋ	off
23. tkíŋ	more
137. to	blue
267. toháŋ kiŋ	wherever
272. toháŋ pi	aside

12. tohán	how
252. tohánča	romantic
297. toknA	direct
18. toká	where
745. tokáhe	newly
16. toké	why
292. tokéšni	thereby
17. tokéya	when
30. tokéšiceye	sorry
257. tośí	younger
209. toxán	several
646. tošpána	bananas
500. tuwéča	anyways
41. táku	great
213. tákȟo	somehow
412. téča	raw
25. tókšin	never
330. tókȟa	anytime
465. tótȟapi	luckily
180. tȟaté	bigger
554. tȟanhán	organic
81. tȟanka	dear
332. tȟankÁ	massive
261. tȟankál	delicious
298. tȟanní	wide
86. tȟaní-tȟokéya	anymore
85. tȟaní-wašte	important
518. tȟaníč'un	domestic
277. tȟo	prime
546. tȟokáhe ókihi	mainly
92. tȟokáhe	full
345. tȟá,	particularly

162. tȟátAŋka	huge
197. tȟáŋka	large
127. tȟáŋčhiyA	strong
131. tȟéčawe	busy
192. tȟíkȟa	heavy
737. tȟókA	numerous
119. tȟótA	longer
483. t'óka	vain
764. uŋkíčheya	ernest
769. uŋmákičheyan	unarmed
679. uŋpičhiyA	associated
151. uŋžíč'ipeya	hungry
339. wadé	everyday
329. wahákȟA	mighty
559. waháŋna	representative
602. wahíyaye	legendary
296. wahíŋyaŋ	merry
582. wahónapi	heavenly
210. wahóta	clearly
205. wahčáŋ	fuckin
138. wakní	definitely
238. wakáb	kinda
59. wakáŋ	together
143. wakáŋčhA	simple
134. wakí	completely
561. wakíhu	modest
507. wakíč'uŋ	secretly
534. wakíčaŋ	honorable
536. wakíčhakič'a	immortal
665. wakíŋhdiyaŋ	aged

729. wakšíčhala	celebrated
191. wakȟáŋ	extra
722. wakȟáŋžiče	civilized
294. wakȟéčha	precious
499. wanaží	handy
601. wanaǧi	destined
544. wanáyiŋ	conscious
248. wanáǧi	downstairs
344. waníć	plain
124. waní	quick
21. waníyaŋ	really
34. waníyetu	first
736. waníyetuštala	potentially
214. wapȟá	natural
752. wapȟé	drugged
774. wayákičheya	glowing
504. wazí	imperial
443. wazíyaŋ	northern
218. waóniyaŋ	criminal
256. waúŋ šnáše	likely
288. waúŋ ye	mostly
264. waúŋ	particular
280. waúŋspe kiŋháŋ	modern
286. waúŋspe	properly
300. wačhiŋyuhá	successful
282. wačhiŋyuhápi	extremely
121. wačhíŋla	calm
247. wačhíŋyAši	exciting
266. wačhíŋye	positive
97. wačhíŋyeyA	clear
230. wačhíŋčala	social
689. wačiŋčiŋyáŋ	sounding

168. waŋbláke	everywhere
216. waŋblí	fantastic
719. waŋgláke	programmed
723. waŋkátu	peacefully
268. waŋná	regular
358. waŋnáke	forth
274. waŋní	awake
495. waŋuŋka	risky
450. waŋyáŋ	immediate
103. waŋyáŋg A	safe
122. waŋyáŋka	wonderful
117. waŋyáŋkapi	quiet
110. waŋzí	glad
532. waŋíčaŋ	mutual
90. waŋčhékhiye	free
141. waŋší	lovely
354. waŋži	distant
130. waŋží	amazing
187. waŋžíla	following
741. waŋžíčhA	sane
664. wašte yútA	spicy
88. wašte	able
384. waštá	commercial
395. waštákečha	nicely
15. wašté	good
386. wašték	jumping
369. waštékatA	intelligent
389. waštéki	eternal
349. waštékilA	generous
387. waštékiya	typical
396. waštékáŋča	random
147. waštélA	normal

224.	waštélakapi	comfortable
392.	waštélawapi	peaceful
26.	waštéwalake	very
375.	waštéwaŋ	minor
72.	waštéwi	beautiful
382.	waštéwóoki	divine
379.	waštéyA	scientific
390.	waštéya	moral
385.	waštéyapi	thirsty
563.	waštéča	automatic
370.	waštéčaka	favourite
353.	waštéčake	pleasant
341.	waštéčha	attractive
383.	waštéčhake	fascinating
391.	waštéčhapi	sandy
381.	waštéȟčA	absolute
639.	wašákA	sufficient
65.	wašík	yet
171.	wašíču	otherwise
279.	waȟpé	decent
676.	waȟéčhe	restored
346.	wenáȟčháŋla	classic
618.	wichá	mini
109.	wikčémna	human
388.	wiówaŋ	fabulous
705.	wičhak'iye	psychiatric
362.	wičhimna	greek
783.	wičhákte	feminine
645.	wičhála	classy
614.	wičháwalakapi	flattered
565.	wičháyapi	alcoholic
333.	wičháŋčhalu	noble

114. wičháša	sweet
314. wičháȟičA	highly
185. wičháȟpi	favorite
701. wičhín	hunted

698. wičhíyakA	competitive
229. wičhíŋčala	female
697. wičhóhaŋ	regularly
331. wičhóiye	online
694. wičhówašte	temporarily
715. wičhówičakaŋ	successfully
637. wičhównA	artistic
154. wičáša	private
787. wišté	partly
484. wolákíč'uŋ	neat
519. wolášte	tasty
521. wolášteča	jolly
788. wonášte	monthly
674. woíci	noted
520. woíyokiphi	legally
58. woíčik'iŋ	best
195. woúŋspe	excellent
523. woǧíŋza	inviting
643. wákpA	rapid
355. wásteya	someplace
290. wáŋlake	directly
63. wí	most
558. wítokšila	relevant
557. wíwičhakičhiyaka	amusing
720. wíyam	colored
704. wíye	carved

474. wíyopiyǎ	shitty
634. wíyuke	antique
685. wíyuskaŋ	elderly
538. wíyuskinyaŋ	biological
555. wíčhaleča	occasionally
669. wíčhoka	rational
666. wíŋyakA	preferred
377. wíŋyaŋkiyA	extreme
543. wóeyawiya	terrifying
323. wóglake šni	unique
321. wóglake	shy
430. wóhanble	magical
398. wóhoye	screeching
366. wóiyokiyA	reasonable
588. wóiyukhaŋ	surrounding
778. wóičhake	exquisite
172. wóičuŋze	innocent
690. wókAšila	snarling
501. wókağe	outer
196. wókiksuye	responsible
152. wókisaŋ	third
505. wókičhuŋyaŋ	convenient
281. wóksape	grateful
576. wólayapi	developing
508. wóokčaŋ	almighty
347. wóowacákiȟi	financial
688. wóowaza	cunning
334. wóoyawaŋ	civil
658. wópičhinhna	discreet
350. wóslolye	religious
397. wótkȟokila	driven
50. wóuŋspe kiŋ	kind

8. wóuŋspe	right
724. wóuŋspekhiya	employed
318. wóuŋspekte	useful
528. wówaksa	elegant
535. wówaksiča	convincing
324. wówakȟe	potential
365. wówapi wóyakapi	downtown
503. wówače	technical
650. wówačhiŋyaka	heroic
481. wówaŋyaŋg	corporate
492. wówaši	practicing
128. wówašte	general
696. wówighta	authorized
661. wówičak'iye	righteous
670. wówičhakA	definite
675. wówičhikaŋ	echoing
789. wóyakhi	likewise
184. wóyatke	fresh
641. wóyukiŋyaŋ	intellectual
155. wóyute	especially
203. wóyuza	local
202. wóyuzaža	german
744. wóčhekiya	apparent
717. wóčhuŋkiyaŋ	audio
250. wóŋyaŋg wačhíŋyuhápi	professional
530. yamníkaŋ	triple
469. yawá	content
104. yašpáŋ	perfect
45. yeháŋni	always
136. yuhá	certainly
64. yuháŋ	happy
611. yuwíŋyaŋ	listed

163. yuzáŋzA	stuck
402. yáyaŋka	wailing
157. zi	green
533. zičá	blond
265. ziŋtkála	golden
335. ziŋtkáluta	orange
91. ziŋtkȟóški	cool
239. zí	bright
312. zítka	pink
399. zíz	blonde

228. zíŋtka	brilliant
610. Ýápi	rapidly
60. éca	thus
633. ékŭŋškaŋ	thoroughly
61. éthúŋ	hence
67. étuŋwaŋ	tomorrow
445. éya	independent
77. éçháŋ	exactly
376. éčhA	worthy
73. éčhetu	probably
236. éčheča	recently
683. éčul	utter
295. ítkala	spoken
449. íwaŋyaŋ	questioning
458. íyaŋ	elsewhere
372. íyašiŋ	smooth
440. íye	constant
424. íyokipazo	torn
414. íyušpus	appropriate
556. íčhiyutȟaŋ	promising

227. íčhupi	aware
651. íŋmamA	chewing
204. íŋyaŋ	main
635. íŋyaŋmA	nude
667. ížaskaŋ	superb
299. ðitke	rare
315. ðáŋ	previously
55. ókac'aŋ	same
89. óksiŋ	high
111. ókskA	cold
427. óma	catholic
311. ómakiyA	emotional
415. ómakȟaŋ	constantly
459. ómani	martial
652. ómazAŋ	atomic
426. óniyaŋ	chemical
413. óyuspa	fond
626. úŋ	combined
654. úŋkík'A	increasing
672. úŋzAŋ	entertaining
497. čhantó	somewhat
553. čhaŋkál	youngest
487. čhaŋkíč'uŋ	kindly
278. čhaŋté čhoŋ	capable
176. čhaŋté	apart
511. čhaŋtéwaste	dearest
169. čhaŋtéwašte	grand
493. čhaŋtéšila	genuine
510. čhaŋzi	sleepy
156. čhetáŋ	french
471. čhetúŋ	oldest
74. čhiyè	young

673. čhiŋkásaŋ	realistic
336. čhwayáya	hopefully
509. čháŋ	woody
714. čháŋpi wičhówašte	diplomatic
655. čháŋtóhphüska	cheerful
686. čháŋzi	gradually
186. čhékpa	however
463. čhéyaŋ	adorable
411. čhítȟola	enormous
775. čhíŋsasa	gigantic
148. čhíŋčhA	personal
241. čhó	harder
630. čhókaŋ kte	banned
727. čhóni šké	surprisingly
786. čhúŋ	butch
208. čhúŋka	tight
748. čhą́	juicy
644. čuŋwíŋyakA	acceptable
29. číkiya	little
234. čík'ala	tiny
101. číŋšma	small
785. jži	repeatedly
235. šahíya	spanish
225. šapȟá	brown
564. šiyohe	legitimate
52. šiyé	enough
406. šiča	burnt
159. šičhá	evil
361. škáŋškáŋ	incredibly
2. šni	not
393. štanžaŋ	internal
624. štēčhiya	reserved

106. šá	red
363. šápe	gray
317. šéyA	solid
46. šíčala	long
472. šíčamna	mere
513. šíč'utȟaŋka	rarely
498. šíč'uŋ	slight
53. šúŋka	today
373. š'íŋ	precisely
750. ųží	repeated
242. žuŋkála	ill
275. ȟečháŋ	firm
410. ȟtayetu	magnificent

3. Index of Words (English)

amusing	557. wíwičhakičhiyaka
ancient	233. iwáŋ
anonymous	466. iyéčhala
antique	634. wíyuke
anymore	86. tȟaŋí-tȟokéya
anytime	330. tókȟa
anyway	80. nážiŋ
anyways	500. tuwéča
anywhere	142. hókšaŋ
apart	176. čhaŋté
apparent	744. wóčhekiya
apparently	189. kté
appropriate	414. íyušpus
arctic	781. thókA
around	47. išná
artistic	637. wičhównA
as	14. kiŋháŋ
ashore	751. mošpó
aside	272. toháŋ pi
asleep	190. iyéčheca
associated	679. uŋpičhiyA
atomic	652. ómazAŋ
attacking	477. iyéya
attractive	341. waštéčha
audio	717. wóčhuŋkiyaŋ
authentic	684. ožáŋžaŋ
authorized	696. wówighta
automatic	563. waštéča
automatically	738. akíču
awake	274. waŋní
aware	227. íčhupi
awesome	179. taŋyáŋ

awhile	540. lechel
back	108. ohúŋ
backstage	779. iwá
backwards	441. akíŋ
baked	623. owótȟuŋ
bananas	646. tošpána
banned	630. čhókaŋ kte
bare	489. t'óče
barely	246. léčhaŋ
basic	360. owályaŋpi
beautiful	72. waštéwi
beautifully	568. owáekiyapi
before	38. mahé
best	58. woíčik'iŋ
better	43. iyéyapi kiŋ
bigger	180. tȟaté
biological	538. wíyuskinyaŋ
blank	490. owájikale
blaring	529. owíkič'aŋka
blind	201. isnáȟna
blond	533. zičá
blonde	399. zíz
blue	137. to
bold	494. ohíye
bound	322. okȟátA
briefly	797. ičhíŋčhaŋwiyé
bright	239. zí
brilliant	228. zíŋtka
broad	451. phézi
brown	225. šapȟá
burnt	406. šiča
busy	131. tȟéčawe

butch	786. čhúŋ
calm	121. wačhíŋla
capable	278. čhaŋté čhoŋ
carefully	259. oyáŋkA
carved	704. wíye
casual	585. lečháŋ

catching	418. kȟáŋ
catholic	427. óma
celebrated	729. wakšíčhala
central	276. okšíčha
certainly	136. yuhá
cheerful	655. čȟáŋtóhphüska
chemical	426. óniyaŋ
chewing	651. íŋmamA
chosen	304. aȟakyápi
civil	334. wóoyawaŋ
civilized	722. wakȟáŋžiče
classic	346. wenáȟčháŋla
classical	570. iyóšiča
classy	645. wičhála
clear	97. wačhíŋyeyA
clearly	210. wahóta
clever	269. stéya
closely	455. akím
cold	111. ókskA
collective	761. ič'íŋyaŋ
colored	720. wíyam
combined	626. úŋ
comfortable	224. waštélakapi
comic	452. ayútaŋ

commanding	763. ičá
commercial	384. waštá
common	199. owówa
competitive	698. wičhíyakA
completely	134. wakí
compound	566. opȟéyatka
compromised	600. owášté
confident	374. okȟóȟi
confidential	548. oíhimna
conscious	544. wanáyiŋ
consistent	539. kiŋháŋl
constant	440. íye
constantly	415. ómakȟaŋ
contained	607. owáktomni
content	469. yawá
continuing	619. ikčháŋ
contrary	423. akís
controlling	583. niyúŋka
convenient	505. wókičhuŋyaŋ
convincing	535. wówaksiča
cool	91. ziŋtkȟóški
corporal	454. owáŋgaye
corporate	481. wówaŋyaŋg
correct	211. hokšína
cosmic	653. oieyapi
courageous	782. akíčheya
cozy	695. oyúspaŋ
criminal	218. waóniyaŋ
cultural	542. owáyakapi
cunning	688. wóowaza
curious	283. ičháŋčha
curly	708. háškaŋ

currently	*436.* háŋtaŋhaŋ
daily	*320.* anúŋpe
daring	*728.* iyúha ale
dark	*132.* imá
dear	*81.* tȟaŋka
dearest	*511.* čhaŋtéwaste
decent	*279.* waȟpé
deeply	*289.* amášoŋ
definite	*670.* wówičhakA
definitely	*138.* wakní
deliberately	*562.* owíthukča
delicious	*261.* tȟaŋkál
delightful	*577.* iwízi
demanding	*593.* inážiŋ
democratic	*632.* oyáte wiwóŋspe
dental	*660.* itȟúŋkaŋ
destined	*601.* wanaǧi
detected	*725.* naye
developing	*576.* wólayapi
differently	*416.* iyóyo
diplomatic	*714.* čháŋpi wičhówašte
direct	*297.* toknA
directly	*290.* wáŋlake
discreet	*658.* wópičhinhna
distant	*354.* waŋži
divine	*382.* waštéwóoki
diving	*628.* híŋhaŋ kísuyapi
domestic	*518.* tȟaŋíč'uŋ
down	*24.* ištáŋ
downstairs	*248.* wanáǧi
downtown	*365.* wówapi wóyakapi
dramatic	*351.* haȟá oyúsaza

drawn	*419.* iȟápta
driven	*397.* wótkȟokila
drugged	*752.* wapȟé
dry	*226.* oíhȟaye
due	*207.* koté
dynamic	*753.* iȟtáŋ
early	*123.* kiní
echoing	*675.* wówičhikaŋ
economic	*514.* owíyokiphi
efficient	*599.* owáhiyeya
elaborate	*711.* ičhóhotapi
elderly	*685.* wíyuskaŋ

eldest	*730.* hiŋháŋla
electrical	*502.* kíčijašká
electronic	*488.* kíčiwíčhakča
elegant	*528.* wówaksa
elementary	*700.* iwičhoŋ
elite	*580.* owákatuya
else	*56.* nážiŋtku
elsewhere	*458.* íyaŋ
emotional	*311.* ómakiyA
emotionally	*572.* iyókiphi
employed	*724.* wóuŋspekhiya
empty	*183.* olówaŋ
english	*150.* ižáŋgúnaŋ
enormous	*411.* čhítȟola
enough	*52.* šiyé
entertaining	*672.* úŋzAŋ
entire	*140.* ičhíŋčhA
entirely	*316.* aúŋspe

environmental	710. oyáte wačhíŋ
epic	647. olákič'iyA
equal	367. owályaŋkapi
ernest	764. uŋkíčheya
especially	155. wóyute
essential	524. taŋhúškila
eternal	389. waštéki
even	32. hékta
ever	48. héčhe
every	51. makȟóčhe
everyday	339. wadé
everywhere	168. waŋbláke
evil	159. šičhá
exactly	77. éçháŋ
excellent	195. woúŋspe
exceptional	734. owákhiphičhA
exciting	247. wačhíŋyAśi
exotic	596. iyómakhaŋ
experimental	792. owákhičhA
exquisite	778. wóičhake
extended	707. ičiŋkbyA
extra	191. wakȟáŋ
extreme	377. wíŋyaŋkiyA
extremely	282. wačhiŋyuhápi
fabulous	388. wiówaŋ
fair	144. mašíčA
fairly	462. híŋtaŋ
faithful	457. hoȟúŋ
familiar	254. iyÁ
famous	193. owáŋye
fantastic	216. waŋblí
far	78. háŋska

fascinating	*383.* waštéčhake
fast	*112.* iŋyéthaŋka
fat	*164.* pȟó
favorite	*185.* wičháȟpi
favourite	*370.* waštéčaka
federal	*309.* théȟówaŋka
female	*229.* wičhíŋčala
feminine	*783.* wičhákte
final	*170.* owáŋka
finally	*113.* okíyaŋ
financial	*347.* wóowacákiȟi
finest	*433.* icúšte
firm	*275.* ȟečháŋ
first	*34.* waníyetu
fitting	*597.* owašlí
flattered	*614.* wičháwalakapi
flowing	*594.* iyóyakapi
fluid	*537.* mní
following	*187.* waŋžíla
fond	*413.* óyuspa
foreign	*251.* opáwŋaŋ
forensic	*613.* owáčhičhiyA
forever	*139.* okíčhiya
formal	*496.* otéwaye
forth	*358.* waŋnáke
frankly	*348.* sápe
freaky	*739.* háŋska ečhél
free	*90.* waŋčhékhiye
freely	*569.* hokšíče
french	*156.* čhetáŋ
fresh	*184.* wóyatke
fuckin	*205.* wahčáŋ

full	92. tȟokáhe
fun	82. oíyoketekiye
fundamental	687. owápi
funny	96. hiŋ-néča
further	174. híŋhaŋ
general	128. wówašte
generous	349. waštékilA
gentle	357. ištanála
genuine	493. čhaŋtéšila
german	202. wóyuzaža
gifted	712. iwásaŋ
gigantic	775. čhíŋsasa
glad	110. waŋzí
gladly	598. owáyečin
global	417. máni
glorious	491. owíčazi
glowing	774. wayákičheya
golden	265. ziŋtkála

good	15. wašté
gracious	592. owáwašte
gradually	686. čháŋzi
grand	169. čhaŋtéwašte
grateful	281. wóksape
gray	363. šápe
great	41. táku
greatly	677. lila
greek	362. wičhimna
green	157. zi
grounded	604. iyókihi
grown	253. ośkáŋ

guarded	*796.* oíčhíŋla
hairy	*590.* phisíŋ
halfway	*421.* akinl
handsome	*231.* owášte
handy	*499.* wanaží
happily	*407.* iyókhaŋ
happy	*64.* yuháŋ
harder	*241.* čhó
hardly	*212.* okíl
healthy	*271.* piyá
heavenly	*582.* wahónapi
heavily	*342.* oíkčakiyA
heavy	*192.* tȟíkȟa
helpful	*403.* oíwakȟe
hence	*61.* éthúŋ
here	*6.* lé
hereby	*609.* oíyote
heroic	*650.* wówačhiŋyaka
hidden	*243.* ošni
high	*89.* óksiŋ
higher	*255.* akáŋl
highly	*314.* wičháȟičA
hip	*422.* hiŋ
historic	*770.* owáŋčaŋ
home	*40.* thípi
homosexual	*772.* oóyuŋkA
honestly	*223.* apȟéčheyapi
honorable	*534.* wakíčaŋ
hopefully	*336.* čȟwayáya
horny	*526.* kaŋ
hot	*95.* okháŋ
hotter	*740.* khéŋ

how	*12.* tohán
however	*186.* čhékpa
huge	*162.* tȟátAŋka
human	*109.* wikčémna
humble	*460.* okíle
hungry	*151.* uŋžíč'ipeya
hunted	*701.* wičhín
identical	*545.* ostéča
ill	*242.* žuŋkála
immediate	*450.* waŋyáŋ
immediately	*166.* okíȟteŋ
immortal	*536.* wakíčhakič'a
immune	*682.* násape
imperial	*504.* wazí
important	*85.* tȟaŋí-wašte
importantly	*550.* okáhni oíhanke
improved	*622.* owákte
incoming	*606.* iŋzí
increasing	*654.* úŋkík'A
incredibly	*361.* škáŋškáŋ
indeed	*182.* iyótake
independent	*445.* éya
indistinct	*258.* opáčuŋ
industrial	*547.* owíčhathuŋ
infinite	*671.* owíŋkčheča
inner	*432.* iŋyaŋ
innocent	*172.* wóičuŋze
inside	*79.* thiŋháŋ
instantly	*589.* na!
instead	*135.* hówa
instrumental	*512.* owášič'a
intellectual	*641.* wóyukiŋyaŋ

177

intelligent	369. waštékatA
intent	587. owíčha
interesting	145. imá, waŋká
internal	393. štanžaŋ
international	308. itáŋčhaŋyaŋ
invincible	721. owáŋžila
inviting	523. woǧíŋza
jammed	631. háŋpaŋ
joint	327. oíyokiphiye
jolly	521. wolášteča
juicy	748. čhą́
jumping	386. wašték
just	5. iyás'a
juvenile	731. pȟéthuŋ
keen	482. mat'éče
kind	50. wóuŋspe kiŋ
kinda	238. wakáb
kindly	487. čhaŋkíč'uŋ
knowing	206. katé
known	116. kiktel
large	197. tȟáŋka
last	42. owáštensica
lately	232. owákpamni
later	71. ayáš

latest	319. haŋká
leading	306. okȟá
least	83. owáčekiye
legally	520. woíyokiphi
legendary	602. wahíyaye
legitimate	564. šiyohe

liberal	795. oóyuŋke
likely	256. waúŋ śnáśe
likewise	789. wóyakhi
lined	605. oktáŋwaŋ
listed	611. yuwíŋyaŋ
little	29. číkiya
lively	662. eyííniyaŋyaŋ
living	99. niya-wakȟáŋ
local	203. wóyuza
logical	531. oltéwaye
long	46. šíčala
longer	119. tȟótA
loudly	515. owíčhak'a
lovely	141. waŋší
low	178. matȟó
luckily	465. tótȟapi
lucky	115. iyówaŋšičA
magical	430. wóhanble
magnetic	579. iwáhetena
magnificent	410. ȟtayetu
main	204. íŋyaŋ
mainly	546. tȟokáhe ókihi
marine	428. mni
martial	459. ómani
marvellous	629. lila wówašte
massive	332. tȟaŋkÁ
maximum	506. iyétokčaŋ
maybe	37. héčhetu
medieval	768. okíčhizečhepi
melted	743. kȟepA
mentally	549. iyóku
merciful	766. owáŋjičeya

mere	*472.* šíčamna
merely	*371.* išniya
merry	*296.* wahíŋyaŋ
mighty	*329.* wahákȟA
military	*198.* okíčhize
mini	*618.* wichá
minor	*375.* waštéwaŋ
missing	*129.* ookíyapi
mobile	*326.* iȟúŋšičA
modern	*280.* waúŋspe kiŋháŋ
modest	*561.* wakíhu
monthly	*788.* wonášte
moral	*390.* waštéya
more	*23.* tkíŋ
moreover	*776.* eháŋni
most	*63.* wí
mostly	*288.* waúŋ ye
motherfucking	*762.* eškúŋ
moving	*126.* niá
multiple	*435.* owáŋkaŋ
musical	*409.* olówan
mute	*756.* nupȟá
muttering	*636.* oíya
mutual	*532.* waŋíčaŋ
mysterious	*340.* psíč
natural	*214.* wapȟá
naval	*627.* iwóktañi
nearby	*368.* iyópta
nearest	*525.* kičúŋti
nearly	*217.* iwáŋyaŋkapi
neat	*484.* wolákíč'uŋ
neutral	*703.* owóŋspeyayA

never	25. tókšiŋ
new	44. háŋka
newly	745. tokáhe
next	57. eháŋni tȟaŋka
nicely	395. waštákečha
no	1. hiyá
noble	333. wičháŋčhalu
normal	147. waštélA
northern	443. wazíyaŋ
not	2. šni
noted	674. woíci
now	11. leháŋ
nowhere	222. iyúha
nude	635. íŋyaŋmA
numerous	737. tȟókA
objective	560. ihékta
obvious	249. oláȟiŋ
obviously	160. kiye
occasionally	555. wíčhaleča
off	31. tkáyahaŋ
officially	359. oákaŋke
often	153. ečhíŋ
old	49. hók'ila
oldest	471. čhetúŋ
online	331. wičhóiye
only	27. iyápi
open	68. oíyok;atek
openly	794. ičhmúŋke
operating	467. iyóyaŋ
orange	335. ziŋtkáluta

organic	554. tȟaŋháŋ
original	219. owaŋ
originally	516. ičháŋska
otherwise	171. wašíču
out	9. ičámna
outer	501. wókağe
outside	94. iŋyékaŋ
outstanding	574. oíke
over	28. kipáhda
overboard	693. oyéče
overnight	461. oháŋke
overseas	615. okíyakapi
own	54. opȟétȟuŋpi
pacific	486. oyáte wówaši
parallel	733. mnihúŋka
partial	702. owáŋyaŋ
particular	264. waúŋ
particularly	345. tȟá,
partly	787. wišté
peaceful	392. waštélawapi
peacefully	723. waŋkátu
perfect	104. yašpáŋ
perhaps	107. mayáŋke
personal	148. čhíŋčhA
personally	244. miye
physical	273. oȟáte
pink	312. zítka
plain	344. waníć
pleasant	353. waštéčake
polar	765. itonáŋye
polite	439. ečháŋ
popular	291. owále

positive	266. wačhíŋye
positively	777. iyéčel
potential	324. wówakȟe
potentially	736. waníyetuštala
powerful	215. owíŋyahȟa
practically	337. nakúŋ
practicing	492. wówaši
precious	294. wakȟéčha
precisely	373. š'íŋ
preferred	666. wíŋyakA
pregnant	173. thípiya
presidential	735. thókȟuŋkA
pressing	571. makíkčiŋ
previous	380. hapíŋ
previously	315. ðáŋ
primary	473. takú
prime	277. tȟo
printed	603. ipá
private	154. wičáša
probably	73. éčhetu
professional	250. wóŋyaŋg wačhíŋyuhápi
programmed	719. waŋgláke
promising	556. íčhiyutȟaŋ
properly	286. waúŋspe
protective	586. išáŋkhota
proud	149. nišíčA
proven	522. owíčhakič'a
psychiatric	705. wičhak'iye
publicly	791. oyátekičhiyapi
pure	270. snuhe
purely	680. owákičhiyA
questioning	449. íwaŋyaŋ

quick	*124.* waní
quiet	*117.* waŋyáŋkapi
quite	*84.* owákikiye
random	*396.* waštékáŋča
rapid	*643.* wákpA
rapidly	*610.* Ýápi
rare	*299.* ðitke
rarely	*513.* šíč'utȟaŋka
rational	*669.* wíčhoka
rattling	*551.* khéčhiyela
raw	*412.* téča
realistic	*673.* čhiŋkásaŋ
really	*21.* waníyaŋ
reasonable	*366.* wóiyokiyA
recently	*236.* éčheča
red	*106.* šá
regular	*268.* waŋná
regularly	*697.* wičhóhaŋ
relative	*453.* oyáwote
relaxing	*793.* ičhépA
relevant	*558.* wítokšila
religious	*350.* wóslolye
remaining	*470.* iyáŋ
repeated	*750.* uží
repeatedly	*785.* jži
representative	*559.* waháŋna
reserved	*624.* štēčhiya
respectable	*584.* iyókiyapi
responsible	*196.* wókiksuye
restored	*676.* waȟéčhe
right	*8.* wóuŋspe
righteous	*661.* wówičak'iye

ripe	760. iŋčhéyeya
rising	437. osnókiye
risky	495. waŋuŋka
roaring	475. lgáŋtaŋ

romantic	252. toháŋča
roughly	726. tháŋka
ruling	681. ičupi
safe	103. waŋyáŋg A
safely	404. okál'Owa
same	55. ókac'aŋ
sandy	391. waštéčhapi
sane	741. waŋžíčhA
scientific	379. waštéyA
screeching	398. wóhoye
second	75. owíŋžala
secondary	758. iŋkháŋ
secondly	790. iŋŋótħaŋ
secretly	507. wakíč'uŋ
select	692. ičhéčhaŋ
senior	302. okħí
sensitive	325. itztáŋ
sentimental	552. owákahŋ
separate	293. aokħáþe
serial	401. oíyayA
serious	105. oyáte
several	209. toxáŋ
sexual	263. oħáŋ
sexy	260. sapsáċA
shaking	408. asní
shaped	754. iyúspe

sharp	305. stȟáŋkA
shattered	608. okšá
sheer	668. oíyoǧeya
shining	442. lgáŋ
shiny	541. ozí
shitty	474. wíyopiyă
short	146. máza
shortly	420. ištáwaye
shy	321. wóglake
significant	480. owákahni
silent	285. ośmá
similar	307. soksáŋ
simple	143. wakáŋčhA
sincerely	656. ičhómni
sleeping	158. ičhá
sleepy	510. čhaŋzi
slick	784. ičhémnaŋ
slight	498. šíč'uŋ
slippery	732. sápA
slow	161. sáŋni
small	101. číŋšma
smashing	746. thóžA
smooth	372. íyašiŋ
snarling	690. wókAšila
so	4. heči
social	230. wačhíŋčala
soft	240. owíćakiya
softly	434. iyútȟapi
solid	317. šéyA
solitary	709. iŋžáŋžiŋ
solo	456. iwéčhuŋ
some	20. k'iŋ

186

someday	284. ośnayaŋ
somehow	213. tákȟo
someplace	355. wásteya
sometime	303. itȟáŋka
sometimes	93. okȟáte
somewhat	497. čhantó
somewhere	118. okážaŋ
sonic	771. itóŋčhaŋ
sorry	30. tokéšiceye
sounding	689. wačiŋčiŋyáŋ
southern	394. oláŋpa
soviet	429. ozá
spanish	235. šahíya
specially	699. owíčhoŋ
specific	338. hačhá
specifically	464. níyuŋ
spicy	664. wašte yútA
spoken	295. ítkala
steady	328. išnála
still	35. heya
stinking	591. hoǧá
stoned	713. owóčhichiyA
straight	120. kȟóla
stray	638. okáhiŋze
striking	678. owíŋyaŋ
strong	127. tȟáŋčhiyA
stuck	163. yuzáŋzA
stunning	595. iwákin
subtle	578. itȟóthi
successful	300. wačhiŋyuhá
successfully	715. wičhówičakaŋ
sudden	245. ośnaye

suddenly	*165.* okíkta
sufficient	*639.* wašákA
super	*220.* nína wašté
superb	*667.* ížaskaŋ
supporting	*567.* oínažiŋ
supportive	*767.* owaníyeka
supposedly	*617.* owášteče
sure	*33.* híŋhaŋna
surgical	*659.* oowótȟuŋ
surprising	*478.* owášteča

surprisingly	*727.* čȟóni šké
surrounding	*588.* wóiyukhaŋ
sweet	*114.* wičháša
swift	*718.* khukhúš
swinging	*640.* kókipA
sworn	*517.* kíčiwičháŋ
tactical	*749.* ičhékhiphičheya
tall	*262.* oȟáŋke
tasty	*519.* wolášte
technical	*503.* wówače
technically	*378.* owáŋskeya
temporarily	*694.* wičhówašte
temporary	*431.* akíŋyaŋ
tender	*479.* t'ó
terrific	*313.* atá
terrifying	*543.* wóeyawiya
then	*19.* heháŋ
there	*7.* hé
thereby	*292.* tokéšni
third	*152.* wókisaŋ

thirsty	*385.* waštéyapi
thorough	*649.* kéye
thoroughly	*633.* ékŭŋškaŋ
thoughtful	*612.* owáyesica
thus	*60.* éca
tidy	*625.* owíŋyakA
tight	*208.* čhúŋka
tiny	*234.* číkʼala
today	*53.* šúŋka
together	*59.* wakáŋ
tomorrow	*67.* étuŋwaŋ
too	*22.* iyéčhetu
torn	*424.* íyokipazo
totally	*133.* taŋíčhA
touching	*343.* ičháŋ
traditional	*447.* héčhu
triple	*530.* yamníkaŋ
tropical	*773.* itóŋkaŋ
true	*70.* hakíče
truly	*221.* owaŋyákapi
twice	*177.* núŋpa
typical	*387.* waštékiya
ultimately	*527.* taŋišila
unarmed	*769.* uŋmákičheyan
unconscious	*448.* iyómakȟiŋyaŋ
underground	*364.* otȟúŋwaŋ
understandable	*757.* owíyuspa
underwater	*575.* mičhá
unfair	*444.* sní
unique	*323.* wóglake šni
universal	*616.* iyówašte
up	*10.* iyéna

upbeat	*691.* iyáŋžila
upper	*405.* iyohlogde
upstairs	*175.* máku
useful	*318.* wóuŋspekte
usually	*167.* iyáya
utter	*683.* éčul
vain	*483.* t'óka
valid	*747.* thíkičhiyaŋ
valuable	*352.* otȟaŋi
vast	*438.* mahóta
very	*26.* waštéwalake
virtually	*663.* owápi wakȟáŋ
visible	*573.* išáŋhna
visual	*468.* ištíma
vocal	*780.* ičhiní
wailing	*402.* yáyaŋka
warm	*188.* oȟŋíŋ
warmer	*755.* owákitahe
weekly	*706.* awéwotapi iyečhiŋ
well	*13.* t'e
western	*356.* oówaŋyaŋk
wet	*237.* owá
when	*17.* tokéya
where	*18.* toká
wherever	*267.* toháŋ kiŋ
whipped	*657.* iškáŋ
white	*100.* ska
why	*16.* toké
wide	*298.* tȟaŋní
wild	*194.* očhíŋ
willing	*200.* owóšte
wired	*642.* išiyečiŋ

wise	*287.* ksá
wonderful	*122.* waŋyáŋka
wont	*648.* ič'íčhib
woody	*509.* čháŋ
working	*76.* kaǧákapi
worldwide	*742.* sáŋmóŋhaya
worthy	*376.* éčhA
wrecked	*759.* mažó
written	*181.* owáŋ
yet	*65.* wašík
young	*74.* čhiyè
younger	*257.* tośí
youngest	*553.* čhaŋkál

Made in the USA
Thornton, CO
10/21/24 23:07:48

7b7e0282-f6d1-49c0-baf6-56e201d4b740R01